Cameroon.
Governance and Development.

Author
Eric Kayem

SONITTEC PUBLISHING. All rights reserved. No part of this publication may be reproduced, distributed, or transmitted in any form or by any means, including photocopying, recording, or other electronic or mechanical methods, without the prior written permission of the publisher, except in the case of brief quotations embodied in critical reviews and certain other noncommercial uses permitted by copyright law. For permission requests, write to the publisher, addressed "Attention: Permissions Coordinator," at the address below.

Copyright © 2019 Sonittec Publishing
All Rights Reserved

First Printed: 2019.

Publisher:
SONITTEC LTD
College House, 2nd Floor
17 King Edwards Road,
Ruislip
London
HA4 7AE

Table of Content

TABLE OF CONTENT 5

GOVERNANCE AND DEVELOPMENT 1

THEORETICAL... 1
INTRODUCTION 4
GOALS OF THE STUDY 16
FOUNDATION AND SIGNIFICANCE OF THE STUDY 20
STUDY ON METHODOLOGY 25
CALCULATIVE AND CONCEPTUAL FRAMEWORK 44
INTANGIBLE AND THEORETICAL MODELS OR PERSPECTIVES ON
DEVELOPMENT 48
RURAL DEVELOPMENT 52
MODELS OF DEVELOPMENT 56
THE CONCEPT OF GOOD GOVERNANCE 58
DEMOCRACY AND DEMOCRATIC THEORY 62
DECENTRALIZATION 70
FUNCTIONS OF LOCAL GOVERNMENTS IN SOCIO-ECONOMIC
DEVELOPMENT 78
EMPOWERMENT 82
EMPOWERMENT FROM A GENDER PERSPECTIVE: POTENTIAL AND
CONTRIBUTION OF WOMEN IN SOCIO-ECONOMIC DEVELOPMENT. 86
THE REPRESENTATION THEORY 90
CONTEXTUAL OF STUDY AREA 95
PROFILE OF STUDY AREA 100
CLIMATE 105
HUMAN AND ECONOMIC ACTIVITIES 106
Population 106
LAND TENURE: 109
SETTLEMENT: 113
ECONOMIC ACTIVITIES 114
DYNAMISM OF LOCAL GOVERNMENTS IN CAMEROON 120

LOCAL GOVERNMENTS	120
OVERVIEW OF LOCAL GOVERNMENTS IN CAMEROON: A HISTORICAL PERSPECTIVE	121
POST COLONIAL ERA	123
THE ORGANIGRAM (ORGANISATIONAL STRUCTURE) OF THE BRC	126
THE PROCESSES OF DECISION MAKING AT THE COUNCIL	130
THE COUNCIL AND THE CHIEFS	131
THE COUNCIL AND THE STATE	133
CEFAM	134
THE ROLE OF THE BUEA RURAL COUNCIL IN THE TRANSFORMATION OF BUEA:	135
TRANSPORT	136
MARKETS	137
HEALTH	138
SCHOOLS AND COMMUNITY DEVELOPMENT PROJECTS	139
OTHER PROJECTS	141
EMPLOYMENT	142
GENERATION OF FUNDS	143
FACTS INTERPRETATION	**147**
PERFORMANCE OF THE BUEA RURAL COUNCIL:	149
PARTY VIEWS	151
THE SDF PARTY IN COUNCIL	155
THE LOCAL PEOPLE SPEAK	160
PRIORITIZATION OF PROJECTS	165
INCOMPLETE WORKS	167
REPRESENTATIVENESS OF THE BRC	168
THE NATURE OF ELECTIONS	170
HOW ELECTIONS ARE RIGGED	175
WOMEN EMPOWERMENT	176
GENERAL DISCUSSION ON THE PERFORMANCE OF THE BUEA RURAL COUNCIL	178
CONSTRAINTS ON EMPOWERMENT	186
IMPLICATIONS OF THE CONSTRAINTS ON THE DEVELOPMENT OF	190
SOCIO-POLITICAL EXCLUSION	191

DEFICIENCY IN INFRASTRUCTURE 193
THE CONCLUSION **196**
REVISION OF COUNCIL LAW 206
ENFORCEMENT OF THE LAW 208
TRANSPARENCY 208
CONTINUITY 209
DIVERSIFICATION OF THE ECONOMY 211
INVOLVEMENT OF THE CIVIL SOCIETY AND OTHER DEVELOPMENT
AGENTS 212

Governance and Development

Theoretical

This study adopts an interdisciplinary approach to provide an account of why Buea is still backward in terms of socio-economic development. It examines the role of Local Governments (LGs) in rural development in supposedly democratic decentralized systems via the framework of empowerment. In other words, what are the consequences when power is devolved from the central government to the LGs? The study is conducted in the South West Province of Cameroon and in Buea precisely, which has its own peculiarities in both demographic and ecological terms when we closely observe rural areas and its associated concerns. The study argues that political empowerment is a necessary prerequisite in development. This perspective also assumes that political decentralization enhances empowerment which provides an appropriate framework for responding efficiently to the needs of the local populace. This paradigm is rooted in the conviction that authoritarian governments have often failed to reach out to the local people through top-down approach to development. From this perspective, empowerment can boost development by providing capacities, values and avenues for local people to fully participate in decision making and any meaningful effort towards improving their lives. Hence, democratic decentralization is perceived as an engine for development. The results of the study reveal that power has not been devolved in its entirety from the central government to the decentralized units and that the rural masses are still not empowered and therefore do not participate fully in the development of Buea. The results of the study also reveal that in Cameroon, there is decentralization without empowerment. The state has officially espoused democratic ideals but its practicality is absent. Implicitly, what operates is still a state led development paradigm (top-down approach) which has met with failures since the attainment of independence. Analysis of the data on elections used for this study suggests that the Buea Rural Council is not representative of the Buea folk because the council representatives are not the choice of the people.

Introduction

> All the evidence tells us that not to empower [local people] is a tragically missed opportunity, not only to create a more just and more prosperous society, but also to advance rural well-being. (James D. Wolfensohn, as quoted from Serageldin and Steeds 1997: cover page)

Background to the study

The post-Cold War era partly experienced challenging debates and concerns on numerous perspectives, theories and 'deep' differences in opinion (ranging from policies to strategies and approaches) on various dimensions of development. The aim has been to arrive at concrete recommendations for action (Szirmai 2005). The concept of development can be traced after 1945, when Harry Truman made a global call to improve the lot of more than half of the world's population living in destitute and poverty in 'primitive societies'. To salvage the poor and improve their living conditions, Truman proposed what he called 'democratic fair dealing'. By this Truman meant a society where nations would respect the rights of men; where all men have a right to freedom of thought and expression and opportunity to share and participate in the common good. According to him, democracy alone can provide the vitalizing force to stir the people into triumphant action. By this he meant according a voice to local peoples in deciding their own affairs. This Trumanian framework also suggests that politics and economics could work together to achieve development and political freedoms.

However, African states were not so concerned with the issue of development at that time because everywhere, they were involved in liberation struggles and wars of independence from their colonizers. But upon attainment of independence, most African states designed and implemented multi- sectorial strategies aimed at improving conditions germane to their multiethnic societies. These strategies were usually based on 'Five-Year Development Plans' that set targets to be achieved in each sector of the economy. Unfortunately, these 'Five-Year Development Plans' were designed and implemented most often by Paternalistic and Dictatorial One Party and military regimes. The result has been the near absence of some basic services in some rural communities such as schools, health centers, good water supply, and better road networks. Hence, in order to create a balance in development between urban and rural areas, 'many *of these* governments felt that substantial state intervention was required to achieve greater equity and poverty alleviation in rural areas.

Existing literature reveals that most central governments in Africa historically took decisions, designed policies and implemented them without consulting local peoples: those who affect and can be affected in the realization of these policies (top-down approach). This approach more or less failed mainly because of the absence of basic freedoms for local peoples; their exclusion from decision-making processes; and the failure to incorporate local cultures and grassroots concerns in development projects.

By the 1980s, Potter contends that 'development policy reflected a concern for accountability and efficiency, which was translated into limiting the role of the state. Both international donors and governments began looking for alternative institutions to deliver services and foster development in the rural areas' (2004). This has been followed by discourses centered on development paradigms that involve local people in designing, planning,

implementing and delivering projects based on local interests and realities. These discourses are based on the realization that:

> Rural people in most developing countries have been reduced or relegated to the role of passive recipients of any meaningful development strategies and policies which affect their lives. As such they bear the consequences of the outcomes of decisions they know nothing about.

In order to limit state powers in development processes and empower local communities within developing countries, Rodrik (2000) proposes the use of democratized political institutions. According to him, these institutions matter in rural socio-economic development because of the propensity of democratic practices to moderate social conflict and induce compromise. One approach to realize this 'Rodrikian' perspective can be through decentralization. This study focuses broadly on the impact of democratic decentralization on development in Cameroon between 1993 and 2003. Under pressure from donors (primarily the World Bank) on the one hand for an alternative development paradigm, internal public demonstrations in Cameroon in the 1990s and in response to some critical developments on the other, the government of Cameroon undertook some political, administrative and economic reforms. One of these reforms was the democratization of political life, through the introduction of political pluralism in 1990.The government of Cameroon which had enacted law No. 74-23 of 5 December 1974 creating councils decided to democratise the system in order to devolve power to these decentralized units to champion the planning and implementation of rural development. The law on decentralization part 1, section 2, and articles 1 and

2 under the general provisions states: "decentralization shall consist of devolution by the state of powers and appropriate resources to local

authorities; and decentralization shall constitute the basic driving force for the promotion of development, democracy, and good governance at local level".

Local development partly via local institutions was supposedly a scheme to better understand rural communities, and be more responsive to the perceived aspirations and constraints of the rural folk (Santiso 2000: 453). Local Governments were considered to be more successful in promoting local participation and empowerment, democracy and cost effectiveness within the framework of the One-Party System. The devolution of power to Local Governments (LGs) seems to me as one model of development from below adopted by the government of Cameroon.

In appraising the functioning and performance of the LGs as institutions which have been given the responsibility to spearhead rural development, 'Senian' freedom would be used to illustrate the importance of freedom and empowerment in socio-economic development (Sen 1999). In his book *'Development as Freedom'*, Sen explores the relationship between freedom and development, the ways in which freedom is both intrinsic and extrinsic to development, that is, a basic constituent of development in itself and an enabling key to other aspects such as stability and security.

He suggests a focus on what he calls capabilities, that is, substantive human freedom, encompassing processes and opportunities, and for recognition of the heterogeneity of distinct components of freedom. Sen (1999) argues that development consists of the removal of various types of unfreedoms (like political freedom) that leave people with little choice and little opportunity of exercising their reasoned agency. In other words, he argues for a focus on the capabilities of people to do and be what they value. One of the vital points is that one human freedom tends to promote freedoms of other kinds, that is, they are relational. For example, Sen stresses that political freedom (democracy) helps to reinforce others such as economic

freedom. Economic needs are considered by some to be more important than political freedom, but Sen reminds us that democracy, as well as being an end in itself, plays an instrumental role in giving people a voice and a constructive role in shaping values and norms. He thus asserts that political rights, including freedom of expression and discussion, are not only pivotal in inducing social responses to economic needs, they are also central to the conceptualization of economic needs themselves. It is also important to support the effective functioning of democracy, that formal rules are not enough without good democratic practice. My point of interest from Sen's work is the issue of democratic freedom or political rights which are the source of empowerment. This forms the core concept of my work.

Another focus of Sen's work is the role of women in development. Here his assertion is that while improving their well-being is expedient, enhancing their agency is just as critical. One notable illustration is women's literacy and employment levels which are the best predictions of both child survival and fertility rate reduction. This aspect of women empowerment is also discussed briefly in this work to espouse the changing role of women from passive recipients to their gradual involvement and contribution in socio-economic development.

The assumption is that democratic freedom and empowerment are necessary conditions for successful developmental efforts. However, the study also questions whether the concept of decentralization is practical or still remains a theoretical construct. This will be discussed with regards to how representative the LGs are to the rural populace which is related to the nature of elections, and if this is accompanied by empowerment. Therefore, through efforts to investigate and highlight the role of LGs in rural development, the study analyses the concept of empowerment as a core concept central in development. The concept of empowerment is examined in two dimensions:

1. Empowerment of the LG through the devolution of power from the central government, that is, the granting of political, administrative and financial autonomy to the LG;

2. Empowerment of the local masses through democratic political rights.

These, however, will not be discussed separately but will be incorporated into the general discussion. Devolution of power should look like what is presented in the power model below on which I base my arguments and analysis.

This power model is designed from the viewpoint of my personal research interest. The model guarantees representativeness. It illustrates that the LG should be responsible for its actions which are based on the priorities of the people and accountability should be directed to the people. The state should probe in at the evaluation stage and assess the performance of the LG and accord the people the right to cast a vote of non-confidence if they are not satisfied with the input of the LG. The state also should fill the gap where there is democratic deficit in the municipality. When this is ensured, the local people will contribute to the stability of the state.

Goals of the Study

The study aims at investigating the following:

- ✓ The role of the Local Government in the socio-economic development of Buea.

- ✓ Explore the performance of the LGs through an assessment of some projects. Here I will attempt an appraisal of their achievements from actors' perspectives;

- ✓ Examine how representative the Local Government is to the local people of Buea. The nature of elections will be used as the main indicator or a yardstick for measuring the level of representativeness of the LG.

- ✓ Examine the level of political empowerment through democratic performance to demonstrate if decentralization has led to empowerment.

Problem Statement

In line with the current global trend of streamlining the role of the state, the governments of most developing countries have devolved power to grassroots institutions with a view to enhance development. But in reality, such devolutions have in many cases been quite inefficient to achieve this goal. The need to empower the local people responds to the growing recognition that local people in developing countries lack control over resources and opportunity to participate in decision making processes. Unless rural people are empowered to participate in the development process, development efforts will only have partial positive effects if at all they have any positive effect. This thesis investigates the role of the Local Government (LG); explains the dimension of decentralization; and evaluates this decentralization/empowerment in terms of whether LGs have achieved the stipulated objectives of development. It also explores the performance through an appraisal of their achievements within the democratic framework and offers some suggestions to rethink democratic decentralization and empowerment and overcome its drawbacks in Cameroon.

This study attempts to investigate the role which LGs as decentralized public institutions can play in the development process. It recognizes their importance as possible avenues through which the goal of socio-economic change can be realized in the presence of empowerment. However, instituting decentralization is not a guarantee for progress depending on what kind of decentralization is set in place. In this light, I will explore to what extent democratic decentralization has led to devolution of power to the people and in what sense. Thus, in my analysis of the case of Buea I intend to critically explore the process of power devolution and find out why progress in this area is slow (below the expectations of the people). Political decentralization is my focus in examining the implication of empowerment in development, where I

mount a sustained critique of the reality or practical decentralization in the Cameroonian context. Questions directed to the level of empowerment are raised and an attempt is made to provide material to reveal to what extent decentralization has really been achieved and if it has actually led to empowerment and the implication on development.

The study will therefore be guided by the following broad questions:

1. What is the role of the Local Government in socio-economic change?

2. What are some of the achievements of the LG in Buea?

3. How representative is the LG to the Buea folk?

4. Has democratic decentralization as an element of power devolution led to empowerment?

5. What is the impact on development?

In addition to this, some cross-cutting themes, such as gender will be explored.

These will guide analysis where an assessment of these council projects will form the basis.

Foundation and significance of the Study

Studies on rural development have often had a narrow focus, concentrating on the agricultural sector which is the main economic activity in most rural areas in Africa. This study adopts a broad focus on rural development, examining the implication of decentralization on local political empowerment, an element that has been overlooked in studies of rural development. The general trend has been that the state has control of what, when, where and how rural development should be done to improve the lives of rural folks.

Processes of democracy and decentralization are actually in existence in Cameroon (in

policy discourses), but the practicality is what needs to be questioned, and whether decentralization has led to political empowerment.

The study was carried out in Buea, a rural area in the South West Province of Cameroon. The decision to study this area and this particular choice of topic was rooted from its historical status, which inspired me to ask some questions, investigate and come up with answers to the questions. In recent times much has been said, written about the failures of government as implementers of socio-economic growth to reach the grassroots. The importance of democratizing institutions so as to empower the local people has also taken precedence in the development literature (Olowu 1988). One observation is that the problem with the current systems is that public institutions cannot attain a satisfactory level of autonomy to work with the rural people in ways that would promote better performance. There is a feeling that Local Government structures are not able to respond adequately to the socio-economic functions that they are expected to, and yet, decentralization was meant to promulgate and address socio-economic related problems which emerged out of the need for effectiveness and efficiency.

Development forces are gradually gaining grounds in Buea because of the presence of the LG which operates at the grassroots and has the capacity to boost participation, but they are not responding adequately and efficiently to the needs of the local people for reasons that will be discussed in the analysis. Much has been written on rural development but it seems to be having very little effect on the problems it seeks to address – are the rural people empowered? The rationale for this study is therefore rooted in the great discrepancy between policy discourse and practice because one thing is said and another is practiced,

> "The rationale for a study is not the discovery of new elements, as in natural scientific study, but rather the heightening of awareness
>
> for experience which has been forgotten and overlooked. By heightening awareness and creating dialogue, it is hoped [discourse] can lead to better understanding of the way things appear to someone else and through that insight lead to improvements in practice" (as quoted from Creswell 1998: 94)

With a focus on this problem in the field, the views, aspirations, potentials of the most destitute sector of the population and the existing reality of why Buea is what it is will be incorporated, bringing about more accuracy in policy discourse and thereby narrowing the gap between discourse and practice. There is a growing perception that there is a causal relationship between political freedom and development. When a people are deprived of this, it subjects them to unwilling actors and deprives them of a better life.

This work is not only directed at bringing more knowledge to the public and the researcher's benefit, it focuses principally on putting forward practical and sustainable results obtainable by policy makers, planners, donor agencies, and various interest groups in Cameroon, the underdeveloped and developing nations as a whole. It will be of profound importance to the Buea community and for rural peoples' struggles for a better life thereby focusing attention and bringing a solution to well identified local problems. The significance of this study is twofold:

1. First, as a source of reference for professionals and policy makers when they are working to implement new policies; and

2. Secondly, the background information provides insight into the dilemmas of the developing world and Cameroon specifically.

Study on Methodology

This thesis is based on a case study that investigates into a particular case (empirical precision) so that generalizations can be made (Yin 2003). Although case studies are stereotyped as a weak method among social science methods (except for anthropologists who rely much on ethnographic works), Yin credits it as the best method to be applied in situations where human beings are the units of analysis (human beings are the focus of the social sciences) in order to unravel and understand complex social phenomena (2003). The study attempts to address some 'what', 'how' and 'why' questions which are typical of case studies (Yin 2003).

The scope of the study

The study is focused on a period of ten years (1993-2003)[4] to obtain a good assessment of what has been done so far by the Local Government in the development of Buea. The year 1993 was a turning point in the history of Cameroon because it marks the period of the first municipal and council elections in Cameroon.

Selection of study area

Buea was selected because:

- ✓ It is a sub-division consisting of several villages and one of the most neglected sections under the centralized system of government;

- ✓ Buea has the potential to develop other non-agricultural activities as alternative livelihoods. For example, tourism;

- ✓ It represents the country's geographic and cultural diversity;

- ✓ Another important point to make Buea appealing for the choice of this study is its history on the one hand and previous personal knowledge of it since I lived there during the three years of my university education. This fact however did not make the accessibility to the sources of data easy.

Sampling Methods

Due to the vast nature of the area, it was impossible to include everybody in the study population so a sample had to be used. First, a number of villages were selected for an in-depth study, as representative cases, guided by the LGs concentration of project activities. It was also imperative to ensure that respondents in the sample were representative of the study area's population.

The strata constituted

a) Level of education

b) Native/non native

c) Time (different council regimes)

Following the above, gender differences were taken into consideration. It was difficult to ensure gender balance as a result of the fact that women were busier than men with farm work and household chores. This left them with little or no time for such an exercise. Moreover, most women in Buea shied away especially as it is a society where women are still second to men. A simple random sampling technique was used to select informants that were representative of the target population. Nichols (2000) argues that in a qualitative research that seeks in-depth understanding of a particular problem,

a sample size in the range of 30 to 50 is normally enough for a small scale study and 50 to 100 for a large scale. In this study, a total of about 135 questionnaires were administered.

A wide range of sources of qualitative data increases the credibility and validity of the research findings (Pratt and Loizos 1992). Hence, 25 respondents were sought from the municipal council – that is, ten councilors and fifteen workers (there are different categories of workers in the council. Councilors are elected, while the other workers are employed either by the state and are working on secondment or are employed by the council); 10 former councilors where included in the sample, while 20 respondents (ordinary villagers, constituting 15 natives and 5 non natives) were sought from each of 5 villages making a total of 135 questionnaires. However, not all the questionnaires administered were filled out for different reasons which included time. A total of 135 questionnaires were administered to 45 women and 90 men. Finally the total number of questionnaires filled out were 108 – 26 women and 82 men. Majority of the people who got the questionnaires – both men and women- were civil servants (retired and those still in service), graduates, petty traders and some farmers.

Table 1: Gender Representation in the Sample of Administered Questionnaires:

Sex	AF	RF%	

Men	90	66.1	
Women	45	33.9	
Total No of Questionnaires	135	100	

Table two: Filled Questionnaires:

Sex	AF	RF%
Men	82	75.93
Women	26	24.07
Total No of Questionnaires filled	108	100

Interview questions directed to the respondents varied with the projects that they have been benefiting from or should have benefited from. A major factor that was also of utmost importance was the different political parties operating in the LG area. Some questions had to be twisted to shift peoples' minds away from party ideologies and differences. The performance of the council as well as the projects created different impacts to different actors involved so there was a bit of technicality in posing the questions so as not to influence anyone's responses. Three villages without projects were also selected though not in the sample, but as a somewhat control group to get their view.

Data Sources

In order to fill the information gap, a multi-source methodology was applied. Data for this study was collected from two sources - through field work and the review of documents. Yin (2003) presents a multi-source data collection technique as a unique feature with case studies which is the ability to deal with multiple evidences in a particular case. Some of these evidences are documents, interviews and observation. None of these sources has preponderance over the other, they are complementary.

This study adopts an interdisciplinary approach to achieve its objectives. The importance of an interdisciplinary approach to this study is rooted on the grounds that no particular discipline seems to analyse issues of socio-economic development and the politics within a "free society" holistically. I will therefore rely on insights from history, social anthropology, sociology, geography, law, political science, and ecology in this study. A number of tools were used to collect data to be used or employed to enlighten the questions that motivated this study:

Pilot Survey

A pilot survey was conducted in the study area for one week during which I targeted the major areas for data collection. I also arranged for accommodation and consulted the Divisional Officer

(D.O – central government representative) for permission to carry out my fieldwork. Getting to the villages was a bit difficult but I was able to make it with the help of my two assistants, both men resident in Buea, who with the help of a guide in each village, located respondents, booked appointments, and helped in taking down notes. The guides in each village also directed us to project sites. Within this one week discussions were held with the director of CEFAM (Centre de Formation d'Administration Municipal) to get a general overview of the operation of LGs in Cameroon. The chiefs of Molyko and Muea were instrumental in providing information on how they relate with the LG in the municipality.

Primary Data

Primary data sources for this study included personal documents obtained from informants and council files. These documents provided insights on the organization of local governments, their objectives and structure in Cameroon. Other relevant documents were sort. Primary sources also involved the use of interviews in the form of questionnaires. Two types of questionnaires were developed – one type was for the local government officials and one for the

local people. However, there was only a slight difference in the questionnaires and this was helpful in collecting data that was context specific from the perception of the different actors involved.

An interview guide was used for the key informants and follow-up interviews also proved helpful. I had an in-depth interview with the former mayor of the council who headed the council half of the period under study. The present mayor was also interviewed. Talking with both mayors was a strategy to consult, contrast and analyze their perspectives to ensure validity. Language didn't seem to be a challenge during interviews owing to the fact that my research assistants and I could communicate in 'pidgin'.[5] For most of the people who could not read and write they were assisted with the reading and interpretation of the questions in the language they could express themselves better and their answers were written. In order to elicit as much information from the field as possible, the study also employed unstructured focus group discussions with beneficiaries of some projects. These focus groups constituted mostly men.

To complement the data from interviews, questionnaires and focus group discussions, observation was necessary. I went round with my assistants to have a look at some of the major projects.

Secondary Sources

Secondary sources are basically published material, either in book form or articles. Reviewing existing literature on a topic helps to formulate questions on areas that are lacking. This therefore makes literature review a means to an end and not an end in itself because it helps the investigator to develop sharper and more insightful questions about the topic (Cooper 1984).

Much of the information from secondary sources on institutional perspectives on development as well as democracy and decentralization in Africa was obtained from numerous sources including, online research reports, textbooks in libraries (both public and private), and research institutions like the University of Buea library, Local Government Training Centre LGTC (Centre de Formation d'Administration Municipal-CEFAM) archives, Centre for Development and the Environment (SUM) of the University of Oslo, and the University of Oslo library. In addition, many websites were consulted.

Data Analysis

Citing McNeill (2001), he posits that "an interdisciplinary study is a scientific method that addresses scientific phenomena holistically. It involves synthesis of disciplinary and scientific approaches in order to approach a problem." In line with his view, a holistic approach of analysis would be a good option in this study taking into consideration its interdisciplinary nature, the extent of historical specificities and critical analysis to question current dominant perspectives on the issues raised, and equally interrogate various options and alternatives to the current discourse. The analysis will be qualitative in nature, except for some few tables.

Limitations of the Study

Collecting data was not an easy task. Fieldwork was conducted during the rainy season, that is, in July and August which is the heart of the rainy season in Cameroon. Most roads were muddy and inaccessible. Sometimes the heavy storms prevented us from leaving the house in time to meet out appointments. This period is also the busiest cultivation period in Cameroon so most of the respondents were busy with their farm work and other activities and had little time to give us information. In effect, most of the appointments had to be rescheduled sometimes more than once.

The time allocated for the exercise was too short as required by a detailed ethnographic study, whereby the researcher is required to spend about a year or so in the field. However, to curb this shortcoming, vignette studies on this area were used to complement fieldwork.

At the level of the Buea Rural Council (BRC), I interviewed two mayors who have headed the BRC within the period of my study. The former mayor (who served as mayor from 1996-2002), was very welcoming. I actually had difficulties tracing his home. Our intention was to meet with him, tell him my mission and then book an appointment because we thought it would be too prompt meeting with him for the first time and asking for an interview. Of course he is a very busy man. But to our greatest surprise, he was more than willing and prepared to dish out the needed information there and then. I had difficulties talking with the BRC staff because they needed permission from the Lord Mayor before giving me any information. This meant that the mayor would tell them what to say so that they don't betray the state. The Secretary General of the council, who had just been transferred from another region to Buea, and was still blind as to what was going on, accepted to give me some council files and documents which, could help me get the material I needed. To my greatest dismay, while my research assistants and I were seated in his office for him to produce the files, he was called up by the Chief of Service (who is appointed by the mayor), and when he reported back to his office, the story had changed. He couldn't give us any documents until we had talked to the mayor. On this matter it was so easy for the mayor to say no despite all efforts to convince him that the documents were to be used purely for academic purposes. In addition to this, all council staff refused recorded interviews and the mayor was very strict on that. He refused to answer most of the questions we asked and said we had no right to ask such questions which were related to financial expenditures and so on. This leaves us in doubt as to whether their activities are genuine.

I was also refused access to peruse their files especially financial records. I had to rely much on the documents the former Mayor presented, to blend with what I observed and the information from interviews and questionnaires.

Buea is a town of intense party political rivalry. For this reason I made it clear to the respondents that I am not interested in politics but the issue at stake. However, considering the fact that the problem of study (empowerment) has a political dimension, and a very sensitive topic at that, it was difficult to prevent this in a place where people are schooled in different and conflicting political ideologies. On my part, I tried to steer clear of the political arena by being neutral. Though I tried to strike equilibrium between men and women, most women were not willing to involve in such matters. Some were always occupied. So finally I got more men in my sample than women. This is probably a reflection of the fact that the society is still dominated by men.

This study does not pretend to analyze the entire council and decentralization laws in Cameroon. It only concentrates on those sections and/or paragraphs that have a bearing on the aims of the study. For example, the interest is on political decentralization with the implementation of democracy in the 1990s. The study is also limited in its scope and objectives. I acknowledge its narrow viewpoint (concentration on the council as a sole development agent in Buea) and recognize that this work can be developed further in the light of work in other fields, now or in the future. I have omitted any discussion of names for reasons best known to me.

The study is broken down into six chapters. Following this introductory chapter, chapter two reviews some existing conceptions and related theories, while chapter three forms the groundwork for the profile of study area. In chapter four, the dynamics of LG is treated in full coverage with an examination of the process of decision making to determine or evaluate whether there is empowerment or not. Successful projects within the frame of

the study are also discussed. The fifth and central chapter comes to the heart of the matter and systematically delves into analysis of the data which adopts a critical perspective because of the different actors involved. Chapter six is the concluding chapter with some reflections to curb some of the prevailing problems. The study is interdisciplinary in nature because it borrows from different disciplines.

Calculative and Conceptual Framework

Introduction

Many theories have developed in the field of development to explain the different paradigmatic trends, strategies adopted in different situations as well as policy formulation and implementation. The general reasons which account for the persistence of underdeveloped economies and social services in developing countries have been laid down by contemporary writers drawn from different development theories. Though theories are generalizations, the application of development theories in case studies seem to vary depending on contextual differences in economic, social and cultural structures and historical experiences This study would therefore examine those relevant theories and concepts that have a bearing on rural development than general theories on development. Hence, Modernization, Marxist and neo-Marxist theories would not be considered in this study because they seem to apply at the level of the state.

The major argument in my theoretical framework is that empowerment enhances participation and plays a fundamental role in rural socio-economic development. Empowering rural people provides them the opportunities to self actualize in society and at the same time institutionalize their cultures which they so much value into development efforts. Culture according to Bell (1990:7, as quoted from Sackmen 2005) is "the effort of symbol makers to define in a self-conscious way, the meanings of existence, and to find some justification, moral and aesthetics, for those meanings. In this sense, culture guards the continuity of human experience". This reflects the plurality of human culture, community, and characteristics: knowledge, belief systems, and attitudes, mode of life, ideologies, thoughts, rituals and practices which

have to be taken into consideration when designing and implementing projects. Implicit in this respect is the fact that 'cultures are instruments for inter-generational survival, to achieve a set of objectives, and to respond to new developments and challenges in society' (Sackmen 2005). Hence, modern democratic culture (democratic institutions and practices) seems to be one mechanism to achieve rural development.

The centrality of rural development in poverty alleviation efforts in Africa is no longer a matter of conjecture. Over the last couple of decades, there has been a growing awareness in academic and policy making circles regarding the importance of institutions in development. A growing body of empirical work has been confirming the important role played by institutions in a wide variety of dimensions. Cameroon, like most African states, has used parastatals as the principal agents of socio-economic development, but the result has not been entirely successful. Ngwa (2005), in examining the activities of the Upper Nun Valley Development Authority (UNVDA) in the Ndop Region in the North West Province of Cameroon, comes to the conclusion that since these institutions were more or less run by government without rural representatives, they couldn't achieve the expected results. The activities of this institution centered on bringing the benefits of modern agriculture to the local people as well as launch the region on the trajectory of sustained economic and social development which includes introduction of new crops and technology, provision of basic ancillary infrastructure and in general, raise the standard of living of the rural poor. The successes of the project were limited by the autonomy granted them. In effect, their activities were more or less dictated by the wishes of the government according to their interests and priorities.

This chapter begins with an examination of the concept of development and argues that rural areas and rural people remain underdeveloped due to the inability of governments to empower institutions and the local people. It

suggests that if the local people are empowered it will boost participation thereby enhancing and promoting sustainable development.

Intangible and Theoretical Models or Perspectives on Development

The study of socio-economic development stands out to be an interdisciplinary venture. The concept of development is ambiguous because it is subject to a wide range of usages, varying from discipline to discipline. The word implies a positive change, progress, transition, and economic expansion, a move from the simple to the complex, from the inferior to the superior and from worse to better. Chambers (1983) defines development as implying 'good change'. Though the definition of development may not be uniform, it is generally associated with a positive connotation – progress: directed at efforts aimed at improving conditions of life (Peet 1999). Development can either be a gradual historical process of change - immanent development, referring to a spontaneous and unconscious process of change; or a planned rapid change, 'intentional development' (Allen et al, 2000), which forms the deliberate policies and actions of the state or development agencies – deliberate efforts to attain higher levels in relation to set objectives.[6] Allen et al (2000) also point out that development as an idea can apply to any field. In biology, development refers to the stages involved in the progressive growth of a living object from birth to maturity. But in cases where the term is used in relation to human societies, it is focused on poverty alleviation throughout the world (Allen et al. 2000). This has been the concern of the global community. Focus has especially been on how to help developing countries to attain a certain level of development. It entails an effort to combat impoverishment, exploit

alternative livelihood strategies (especially in the rural areas where the main source of livelihood is agriculture).

Though development is intended for the well-being of all in society (raising the standards of living, poverty alleviation), Chambers (1983) contends that some people end up being the losers of such processes. This happens when a peoples' way of life is altered for the worse. In this same line of thought, Törnquist (1999) purports that referring to development as a process where resources are put to 'better use', the phrase 'better use' is varied depending on who is concerned as resources put to use may be advantageous to some and disadvantageous to others. Such resources include natural resources, technology and capital (Törnquist 1999). Reflecting this view therefore, Chambers notes some general points about the idea of development:

1. It should be an all-encompassing change, not just an improvement in one direction; (Chambers, 1983; Jaffee, 1998);[7]

2. It should be a process which builds on itself where change is continuous and where improvements proceed previous improvements;

3. It should be a process that occurs at the social level and in the individual human being at the same time (human development).

His explanation for the third point is that changes in society have implications for the people who live in that society, and in the same light changes in how people think, interact, make their livings and their perceptions form the basis for change in society. This is rooted on the premise that socio-economic change shapes and is shaped by individual perceptions, beliefs, cultural patterns, economic organizations, methods of production and distribution,

socio-political arrangements and the international economy. Implicitly, human development or human capital which is a function of human freedom also boosts societal development.

Rural Development

Rural development is any effort aimed at improving and/or enhancing rural livelihoods in the social and economic domains. It involves both the transformation of lives and landscape to ensure a significant improvement in the quality of life of the rural folk. Thorbecke et al (1992), contend that 'the rural poor, who represent a latent productive potential, need to be provided with an appropriate policy and institutional framework, resource and technology support, and an enabling market environment so that they can raise their productivity on land where access to it is assured, and raise their income through off-farm income generating activities, where there is scope for generation of productive employment'. There can be no other way of achieving this than preparing the rural people with the necessary skills that would permit them to explore other avenues and other activities. Moreover, the success of this lies in the fact that dialogue is created with those who will be directly or indirectly affected by any decisions and actions. Implicitly, decisions and responsibilities should be shared instead of imposing on the people because Mikkelsen (2005) argues that participation is not only a democratic principle, it is a right.

At the Fourth Annual World Bank Conference on Environmentally Sustainable Development, under the theme "Rural Well-Being", Boutros Boutros-Ghali, the then Secretary General of the United Nations, stressed the need for human welfare in rural areas: 'it is in the rural areas that some of the most intractable problems of development are found' (Serageldin & Steeds 1997). He proceeds: '(...) I encourage you in your examination of policies, extrapolating from innovative pilot programs, to promote rural well-being.'

This is in order to realize the goals inherent in the common vision of the international community. To succeed at efforts geared towards rural change, Serageldin and Steeds outline the following important considerations:

1. The need to understand the rural people in their own context – their specific local

conditions, felt needs, constraints and possibilities;

2. The need to design, implement, and evaluate activities with the rural people, not for them, because development is something people do, not something done for them;

3. Channel resources to the rural people as directly as possible and allow them to manage those resources. This can be achieved through promoting an enabling institutional environment – one that fosters representative, decentralized, and participatory local governance in order to create the conditions which the rural populace can more effectively use their own talents and capabilities (1997:52).

Serageldin and Steeds (1997) acknowledge the critical role rural people play in the global effort to encourage sustainable rural development. In this light, it is imperative that rural development and rural well-being be not limited to investment in economic development projects alone. Social services, including education and health, are needed to help people 'develop' as well as critical for rural people to maximize their potential and to reduce rural-urban migration. To achieve these, grassroots drivers of rural development are needed and Local Governments may champion this course of rural development to boost and promote greater participation and governance and build local capacity.

Models of Development

2.3.1 The Participatory Model of Development

Stöhr and Taylor (1981 as cited from Potter 2004) provide an informative overview of development from below. Their account stresses that there is no single recipe for such strategies as there is for development from above. Development from below, he purports, needs to be closely related to specific socio-cultural, historical and institutional conditions. Bottom-top strategies are varied but most importantly they stress the concern for local and community participation in development design and implementation of projects, reducing outside dependency and promoting sustainability.

Alternative development has come to be associated with new and wider conceptualizations of planning and development with its main distinguishing feature being the fostering of participatory development, associated with more equitable principles of growth, where social exclusion inherent in rural areas would be eradicated. And given the long hegemony of the 'top-down', western, rational planning and development, increasing the involvement of people in their own development is imperative. Chambers

[(1983) as cited from Potter 2004)] averred that it was time for the last to be put first. In his context, participation means much more than involvement or mere consultation (Potter 1985). While these calls seem eminently reasonable, the question remains 'how is this to be achieved'? The answer is simple- through democratic rights to participate, and through the devolution of powers to the people concerned.

The Concept of Good Governance

Writing for the World Bank, Landell-Mills and Serageldin (1991) define governance as the use of political authority and exercise of control over a

society and the management of its resources for social and economic development. It encompasses the nature of the functioning of a state's institutional and structural arrangements, decision making processes, policy formulation and implementation capacity, effectiveness of leadership, and the nature of the relationship between the ruler and the ruled.

Different kinds of governance do exist but in many African states the most common are centralized and decentralized governance. The UN 2005 Sachs report on the implementation of the UN Millennium Development Goals argued that poor governance in African states was one of the key reasons for ongoing problems in meeting the goals of development. The principle of good governance was launched in international aid circles at the end of the cold-war as a guiding principle aimed at the internal restructuring of government machinery of developing and transitional economies. It was an approach adopted by the World Bank and aid agencies as a pre-condition to receive development aid, which was concerned with improving the political leadership of democracy and integrating economic and social goals. In effect, it is endorsed as a core element of development strategy (Doornbos 2004).Though adopted primarily as a political policy it was restrictive to the economic sphere.

Doornbos argues that the quality of good governance can be evaluated in terms of its democratic content. Implicitly, good governance and democracy are inseparable, that is, they converge both "conceptually and practically" in the study of practice of the formulation and implementation of public policy (2004). Its landmarks include: accountability, transparency, effectiveness and efficiency; it is also participatory, consensus oriented, equitable and inclusive and follows the rule of law. It ensures that corruption is minimized (like in the case of election malpractices). For good governance to be efficient, democracy must be operational. Expanding democracy-whose indicators include multi- partysm, freedom of speech and the press - improves individual opportunity for prosperity and improved well-being, thus contributing to the growth of the society. And in ensuring effectiveness and efficiency, processes and institutions produce results that meet the needs of society while making the best use of resources at their disposal. The concept of efficiency in the context of good governance also covers the sustainable use of natural resources and the protection of the environment.

The concept of good governance is of importance in this study because it brings out the idea of democracy which gives freedom and empowerment to the people. Here, there is an attempt to establish a link between building good governance (democratic governance) and development, where I very much agree that these issues are not sequential but go hand in hand. The reasons for exploring the concept of good governance are rooted in my interest to draw a focus on the symbiosis between politics and development for a fuller understanding of the problems of development.

Democracy and Democratic Theory

Karlstrom (1996) addresses the concept of democracy as 'a local political cosmology which emphasizes the values of justice, civility and open communication between rulers and subjects', where, according to Schumpeter, political decisions are realized for 'common good' by making the people decide issues through the election of individuals who are to assemble in order to carry out their will (1976). Schumpeter further states that this common good implies providing answers to questions in order that every measure taken can unequivocally be classified as 'good' or 'bad'. It is the rule of the people, depicting liberty, and freedom. Lijphart (1999) gives the following as definitions of democracy: (1) Representative democracy is defined as the government by the representatives of the people; (2) Abraham Lincoln's famous stipulation of democracy as government for the people and by the

people, that is, a government that works in accordance with the peoples' preferences.

There are different kinds of democracy, majoritarian and consensus models (Kaiser 1997:434 as quoted from Lijphart 1999). However, the majoritarian model will be ruled out in this study because it stipulates that the majority should govern while the minorities oppose. Sir Arthur Lewis perceives this model as undemocratic as it is characterized by exclusiveness (Lewis, 1965). This is common in societies with two-party system. The consensus model of democracy requires that a consensus should be arrived at through discursive means (Long 2001). Lewis seems to work in the same line of thought as Schumpeter. In his view, the consensus model depicts the real essence of democracy where all who are affected by a decision should have a chance to participate in making that decision directly or indirectly through chosen representatives. Lijphart (1999) outlines 8 criteria for defining and measuring democracy proposed by Robert A. Dahl. They include:

- ✓ A right to vote,
- ✓ The right to be elected,
- ✓ The right for political leaders to compete for support and votes,
- ✓ Free and fair elections,
- ✓ Freedom of association and expression (civil liberties),
- ✓ Alternative sources of information,
- ✓ Institutions for making public policies depend on votes and other expression of preference.

Democratic freedoms permit political parties to mobilize and draw support on the basis of their preferred espousal interests and identities.

This does not rule out the fact that in a democratic society the management of affairs requires certain special aptitudes and techniques that needs to be entrusted to those who possess them. Yet, this does not have to affect the principle of common good by allowing the people decide issues, because these people who are there (representatives) are simply there to carry out the will of the people. Democratic governments allocate a greater share of responsibility to lower level institutions, the level that benefits the largest segment of the population who are those who live in rural areas. Free and fair elections take the stage in a democratic system where there is socio-political inclusion.

Where there is disagreement in opinions as to which goals are to be achieved, how this could be approached, and the strategies to be employed, opposition springs and this leads to adjustments. A strong opposition party strengthens the party in power and forces it to work to win the confidence of its electorate. It boosts competition and emulation to propagate the name of the ruling party. The implication of democracy is highlighted further by Uslaner (Hooghe and Dietlind, 2003) who purports that democracy admits variety which helps to create a forum for competition. It also permits criticism on which the opposing parties rely on to make improvements.

In the right-based approach to development, a lot of emphasis has been laid on democracy as its absence ushers in less representative political systems with weaker structures for aggregating and arbitrating interests in society (Grindle 1980, Heyden et al. 2004, as cited from Court et al. 2005). In an undemocratic society, policy making processes tend to be more centralized and thus often remote and less accessible with limited scope for wider input or participation. This completely rules out the sense of belonging in the people.

A society's well- being depends on ensuring that all its members feel that they have a stake in it and do not feel excluded from the mainstream of society. With a sense of belonging or inclusion (both political and social), the local people do the best they can to self actualize in society.

Some scholars have tried to question whether democracy actually fosters development by supporting their claim with empirical examples of countries that attained remarkable economic progress under dictatorial regimes (examples include Uganda). Though it is also insinuated that dictatorship might hasten development in most cases based on the fact that there is no time wasted on rivalry and arguments from different parties, I question the relevance of any project imposed on a people because if its not put to use, then, its not development. Dictatorship in most cases breeds conflict, and conflict sometimes constitutes a barrier to development. It also favors minority rule, where the majority of citizens are alienated from the political system. This precludes the citizens from engaging lawfully in economic activities and inhibits citizen participation in decision and policy making (Pereira, 2000). Democratic regimes have precisely the opposite effect and promote development.

Shanmugaratnam, analyzing Sen's capability approach to development presents a contrary view to the authoritarian regime, by establishing a link between democracy and development (see Sen 1999, Shanmugaratnam 2001, Elgström and Hyden 2002). Elgström explores the extent to which democracy or any dimension of it, such as freedom, is beneficial to development (Elgström, 2002). His ideas seem to have the same philosophical roots as Sen, where freedom helps people to participate in decision-making at different levels and permit them to express their economic and other needs. Not only does democracy lead to progress, the latter also generate high probability of democratic government. On another level, Elgström and Hyden (2002) establish the nexus between development and democracy. They reveal that

development promotes democracy when the emphasis on economic development has to be broadened to encompass measures of human development. From both analyses, the following observation can be made: democracy and development are inseparable.

Defining democracy as an "ongoing search for an institutional resolution of the problem of power that lies at the core of politics", Shapiro (2003) in his theory attempts to establish a link between democracy and development. In his view, democracy should be based on a rational collective action and not a majority rule because this will force the minority to become the tyranny. He stresses the role of deliberations in the promotion and achievement of common good. Expanding this nexus wider, levels of democratic performance will be discussed to explain the extent of democratic output. On democratic performance, Elgstöm pays more attention to certain political events and institutions and the nature of elections.

Decentralization

Mahatma Ghandi, architect of Indian independence, advocated

> "swaraj" or self- rule, which implies the rule of the people. This concept forms the basis of democratic decentralization and the establishment of 'panchanyati raj' – (peoples' council) institutions in India. The objective is to strengthen the institution of self- government at the village "taluk" and district levels. It is built upon the premise that, all "power" in a democracy rightfully belongs to the "people." Thus, the essence of democracy lies in empowering the

people to govern their own affairs by themselves within their jurisdiction. The emerging trends in recent years are the decentralization and devolution of powers to the local [government and people at various levels.

Decentralization is a step to promoting democracy. It is the transfer of responsibilities, in the management of local affairs, from the central government to the local government. The purpose is to bring administration closer to the people, and this has proven to be the better way to improve the living standards of the population. Local communities stand out to be the principal pools of local development. They are political laboratories that are inevitable in the fight against poverty and the implantation of democracy. There are four different kinds of decentralization but I will be primarily concerned with two which are important to my study.

- ✓ Deconcentration: designates an administrative process of decentralization of resources whereby the local services remain under the control of the central government. Eriksen et al (1999) refer to this as administrative decentralization. The transfer of authority is from the central government to local "branches" of central government (Eriksen et al. 1999). In this context the participation of the local population is only a tool in the accomplishment of projects. Hence, it is a form of centralization in disguise.

✓ Devolution: This on the contrary is the delegation or surrender of powers of the central government to local authorities (Mukete 2004, Harriss et al. 2004, Eriksen et al. 1999), or institutions which are based on local political representation (Eriksen et al. 1999). It could also be referred to as political decentralization and this means that the institutions to which this power is devolved must be governed by locally elected persons.

Citing the deficiencies in centralised models of governance, Eriksen et al (1999) posit that decentralization was seen as an alternative model of governance and is therefore referred to as part of the solution and an answer to the need for more involvement and participation of local communities in development processes. It is also a remedy to the problems of power abuse,

mismanagement and bureaucracy. Participation in decision-making and implementation and information of the local population seem to be some of the objectives devolution. Devolution permits at least in theory, more participation, transparency and accountability in the management of public affairs.

Decentralization stands out amongst the priorities of the African traditional agenda because it empowers local institutions thereby enhancing and modernising democratic societies and states in Africa. By enforcing accountability, it lays the ground for monitoring and hence potential sanctions, both positive and negative. And accountability automatically becomes a responsibility in the normative sense of the word. But who these decentralized units have responsibility to is a challenge we need to find out.

Political decentralization or devolution is the more real form of decentralization and the whole idea of this work is based on devolution of power. Though some disadvantages are linked to this such as inequality between districts and local authorities (Eriksen 1999), I will also challenge any argument that states that this does not happen in centralized systems because the inequality between regions, cities and rural areas today especially in African states was created during state led development. When the local people are given the formal power to decide how problems should be dealt with they get more involved. The question that arouses my interest here is, 'Was democratic decentralization a government mechanism to strive to establish its strong administrative presence at the local level, or was it meant to serve as an instrument for local interests vis-à-vis the central government?'

Advocates of decentralization in developing countries argue that it brings government closer to the people and hence, be more responsive and more likely to develop policies and outputs which meet the needs of the ordinary people. Responsiveness has to do with the degree of empowerment and ownership felt by those affected by them, and this is determined by the

effectiveness of institutional and public accountability mechanisms. However, the degree and type of decentralization existing in a system will determine this outcome, that is, the outcome is dependent on regime type (Crook and Sverrisson

2001). Considering that the majority if not all of the people in developing countries are excluded from politics (because power is concentrated in the hands of a few), any scheme which offers greater political participation by ordinary citizens at the grass-roots seems likely to increase their voice and hence, the relevance and effectiveness of government's developmental output. Such is the case with decentralization. But an important question to be asked here is: 'was this a scheme meant to benefit the people or was this scheme perpetuated by state undercover interests? This question arises out of Crook and Sverrisson's observation that different governments do have different political purposes and motives for introducing decentralization reforms and that these purposes are embodied in the details of the structure and form of the decentralization scheme, which are revealed in the way the system functions after the introduction of decentralization. This however is not the focus of this study but gives us a clue to some motives behind decentralization which is why there is a discrepancy between what is said and what is practiced.

The three concepts above – good governance, democracy and decentralization are relevant to this study as they usher us to the main concept of the study – empowerment. Good governance has been used here to demonstrate that in a democracy, people are empowered and can therefore make choices and their voices heard. Decentralization is a means of bringing this democracy, devolving power closer to the people at all levels of society especially at the grassroots. In this regard, decentralization and democracy are elements and indicators of good governance, hence, the three frameworks are interrelated, where decentralization and democracy are perceived as development-promoting form of governance. The Local Government is thus a decentralized political unit that may promote well-being at the grassroots level.

Functions of Local Governments in Socio-Economic Development

The move towards democratization and decentralization has added new roles and responsibilities on the LGs. When governance is actually transferred to the LGs, it provides significant opportunities for popular participation and increased involvement by the people and communities in decisions that directly affect their lives. Moreover, it is through the empowerment of LGs that municipal programmes, plans, and service provisions have a higher likelihood of reflecting local needs more accurately than in centralized systems of governance (Materu 2001). Olowu (1988a) in analyzing the prosperity of Zimbabwe in the 1980s, attributes this partly to the Local Government institutions – both urban and rural councils. Their contributions included the provision of basic social and economic infrastructures that support other development activities. The councils are filled through multi-party elections, and are responsible for a wide range of services both of economic and social types amongst which are housing, health, education, social welfare, sewage, water, refuse collection, and sometimes electricity

In the consultative group meeting to discuss the reconstruction and preventive strategies of the Hurricanes Mitch and Georges which caused devastating damages on the countries of Central America and the Caribbean (Friday 1999), the LG was seen as a pioneer in national reconstruction, future disaster mitigation, and economic and social development in ways that ensure greater participation of all segments of society. This is based on the assertion that local governments possess specific potential comparative advantages in preparing for and recovering from disasters based on the reasons outlined below:

-Local leaders are prone to better understand local situations, and local governments, especially mayors, if provided with adequate resources and autonomy can provide critical leadership concerning decisions on resource allocation. Their day to day knowledge of local resources, local needs and other community factors provide them with insights and capacity for making sound and more timely judgments than central governments. Citizens look to their elected officials (?) for immediate responses to their problems. In many arenas, Local Governments execute certain expenditure programs better than national governments due to their physical proximity to the community which gives them a better capacity to determine and assess local interests and requirements.

- Jager (1997) also contends that Local Governments have the ability to provide services more efficiently and cheaper compared to central governments. Citing the example of El Salvador, the analysis points to the fact that many public works were implemented by municipal governments at costs from 'one-third to two-thirds lower than when the same types of works were executed by central government agencies. The reasons for this include: greater control over work crews, closer supervision, and shorter travel distances to work sites, scrutiny by the electorate and greater accountability by elected and appointed local officials'. This highlights the advantages inherent in local level decision-making, service delivery and control. The capacity of LGs to mobilize local resources cannot be over emphasized. Because they can more accurately reflect local priorities, they can also more accurately develop a sense of accountability among their constituencies. More still, LGs ensure that local processes are democratic and good democratic practice at the local level greatly improves construction, reconstruction and service delivery. Attuned to voters' needs and reactions, local governments have the potential to build community consensus around controversial issues, including infrastructure building, and other environmental programs.

In sum, this is to reveal the ability of LGs to act generally as catalysts to economic and social development. This general notion of the contribution of LGs in socio-economic change will provide a basis for the evaluation of LGs in Cameroon if they are structured to function in an adequate manner and if their performance meets the expected standards.

Empowerment

Barnes conceives of power as one of those things which makes its existence apparent to us through its effects, and hence it has always been found mush easier to describe its consequences than to identify its nature and its basis (Barnes 1988). Basing on political power, he draws a line between empowering and authorizing. He elicites the fact that when an agent is empowered, discretion in the direction of a body of routine activity is transferred to him, which actually results to his possessing it. The empowered, though expected to further the objectives of the power holder, does this only when such objectives are concordant with the whims of the masses. In so doing he formulates his own plans, in negotiation with those under his care and puts them into action independently without interference from the power holder. This projects empowerment as a simple and adaptable method of mobilizing a capacity for action and keeping it operative, while authorizing confers mere authority.

Most works on empowerment have been limited to its definition that focuses on giving people the opportunity or ability to invest in their health and education and to shape their lives by being able to participate in the opportunities provided by economic growth and have their voices heard about decisions that affect their lives. These works have also focused on access to essential public services, such as health, education and safe water. Most of all, the target has been women since they are presented as the most vulnerable in society and most poverty stricken as their potentials were undermined and

they were relegated to the background in the social and economic spheres. Hence, literature has often limited the element of empowerment as one-dimensional, focusing on self efficacy of women (Conger and Kanungo 1988). Have we ever asked ourselves what a society we would have if everybody (both men and women) are given the opportunity to be heard about decisions that affect their lives, that is, if people are politically empowered, what effect would this have on development? In other words, instead of participation and involvement becoming a source of empowerment, how can empowerment boost participation and the involvement of all?

The concept of empowerment is briefly discussed because it is all implied in the above concepts and theories (good governance, democracy and political decentralization). However, I wish to draw attention to the slight difference in my treatment of this concept to clear the doubts off the mind of the reader. It will be treated as a core concept in this study, and focus is on political empowerment which is purported by Pyne (2005) to be a situation where people are free, and have the strong political motivation to make positive changes (democratic rights). It is a situation where the common folk are given the opportunity to enjoy equal privileges to make unbiased choices on their own. Although development is an element of empowerment, I also hold that empowerment is the centerpiece of development with regard to the fact that it gives people the freedom (about everything that promotes wellbeing) to express their choices. Empowerment is therefore used here to embrace autonomy of the LG and the people.

Empowerment from a Gender Perspective: Potential and Contribution of Women in Socio-Economic Development

Over the past decades, women all round the globe, have been completely excluded from any development effort, albeit in varying degrees. In African societies, the situation is worse. Boserup explains the inability of women to get involved in such projects to their lack of qualification, a trend that started right from the colonial days where according to her, 'the curricula of missionary schools for African girls laid more emphasis on domestic activities' (1970:122).Even in the pre-colonial days, girls were not even allowed to go to school, they were subjected to the role of housekeepers. It was held that an educated woman stood little chances of having a husband and in the African context it was stigmatizing to find a woman at a certain age still in the house of her parents, or unmarried because marriage was a norm for girl children (Boserup 1970). In effect, cultural and societal norms deprived the woman of exercising her intellectual and management skills which till date are barring a multitude of women from certain opportunities to work in the social and economic sectors. This has reduced women to working only in the agricultural domain which is dominantly family-based. Boserup points out that more women are engaged in agriculture than men especially in societies where agriculture is not mechanized.

The contribution of women in socio-economic change cannot be overemphasized. They are blessed with special knowledge and talents in managing their homes, engaging in activities concerned with their children's school, they hold their families together. Though a high proportion of women are engaged in agriculture (over 80%), they are gradually finding ways of improving their lives by diversifying the economy. Diversifying the economy provides the foundation on which a society can create employment and raise living standards as noticeable in western societies. Women are gradually shifting from subsistence activities for family use to commercial production for sale and small scale market trade and services. These women rely on their initiatives for generating income for their enterprises and make remarkable contribution to the economy through self-employment and wage. Although Buea is still at a low stage of development, the extent to which women have penetrated the arena of development must be considered large when perceived in line with this low level of development and the level of empowerment.

Women are gradually being absorbed into positions of leadership and white collar jobs. An example is the third deputy mayor of the Buea Rural Council who is a woman, and a handful of female councilors, one heading the educational committee of the council.

Though the seclusion and exclusion of women in decision making and in the service sector is losing its grip, the proportion in relation to men in other occupations and in decision making is low. This low rate of female participation is still consistent with men's pattern of categorizing women as the weaker sex, and the inability of women to measure up with the men because of the gap that had already existed. Moreover, men as policy makers only design policies that subject women to second class citizens. Therefore, women are still marginalized. As such, it will be important to find out if the achievements of the BRC present different consequences for men and women.

The Representation Theory

Pitkin (1967) observes that in modern times everyone wants to be governed by representatives, either individuals or institutions.[8] But what is the idea behind representation, and what expectations do voters have of representatives? Pitkin explains that representation is used as a device to furthering local interests, as a control over the power of the state. Representation means popular representation, and to be linked with the idea of politics, of everyone's right to have a say in what happens to him/her.

What makes people feel represented? When is it correct to say that they are represented? What counts as evidence that they are represented? Is it voting, identification? In the midst of the debate as to what representation means, Hobbes (cited from Pitkin 1967) lays down some formal arrangements that accompany representation; (1) Authorization: the representative has to be given the authority to act through voting; (2) Accountability: the representative has to take responsibility to be accountable for his actions. Owing to this attribute, accountability is a precondition for standards that can be practically and effectively applied to derive sustainable development. It can not be enforced without transparency (openness) and the rule of law. An organization or institution is accountable to those who will be directly or indirectly affected by its decisions or actions.

Hence, a vital element that pervades this debate is that a political representation where rights are respected is based on elections. Some theorists argue that a representative's duty is to reflect accurately the wishes and opinions of those he represents, he must do what is best for those in his charge, though sometimes he might use his own judgments and wisdom, since he is chosen to make decisions for his constituents (the relation between representative and constituents).My position is in this same direction.

The application of this theory is to highlight and present a picture of the consequences of a true representative who reflects the choice of the people and the situation when the representative is not considered the peoples' choice. The issue of representativeness of the LG is a major factor in the functioning of the LG.

In sum, the concepts and theories examined above have a profound bearing on the subject or main theme of study – that empowerment and freedom are instrumental or prerequisites in development endeavors because they boost participation and involvement (the latter is also true of the former). The concepts and theories have helped to identify some of the common features which a good decentralized democratic state must possess to be admitted that power has been devolved. The frameworks have also been selected to highlight areas of possible connection for my interpretation. To

that extent, this is an empirical study of a very general kind. The analysis will follow the same pattern to reflect this goal and present the situation of Buea and Cameroon in general.

This chapter is a reflection of the theories that are of utmost importance to the study, from the general concept of development narrowing it down to rural development. Some models of development are introduced such as the participatory model of development. It also introduces the concept of good governance, which is a reflection of core concepts such as decentralization and democracy. These dwindle down to the concept of empowerment. Democratic decentralization which is synonymously used here with political decentralization is treated in this work as the main element of power devolution to the LG (autonomy) and to the ordinary people who should have the freedom of choice and participation. Empowerment of women is also briefly examined because women have been the least empowered, considering their position which is related to their sense of family and community.

Contextual of Study Area

General Profile of Cameroon.

Cameroon is a sovereign state found in West and Central Africa. It is bordered to the North by Chad, to the West by Nigeria, to the South by Congo, Gabon and Equatorial Guinea, and to the East by Central African Republic. Bantu speakers were among the first group to settle Cameroon, followed by the Muslim Fulani in the 18th and 19th centuries. The country escaped colonial rule until 1884, when treaties with tribal chiefs brought the land under German domination. Germany occupied the area from 1884-1919 when she was ousted out of the country by a joint Anglo-French force in 1919. The two forces decided to share the territory, Britain occupying a very small portion (1/5) owing to the fact that they already had many colonies in Africa. The two territories were known as British Cameroon and French Cameroon (Fanso 1989). After World War II, the country came under a U.N trusteeship in 1946, self-government was granted, and the Cameroon Peoples' Union emerged as the dominant party by campaigning for reunification of French and British Cameroon and for independence. French Cameroon gained independence in 1960 and in 1961, the territory of British Cameroon decided in a plebiscite to attain independence by joining French Cameroon, their brothers in the East. The two Cameroons formed what was known as The Federal Republic of Cameroon (that is, British Cameroon became West Cameroon while French Cameroon became East Cameroon) until after a 1972 referendum, when a unitary state was formed out of East (French part of Cameroon) and West (British Cameroon), hence, the new appellation 'The United Republic of Cameroon'. In 1984, the word 'United' was dropped and the country became La 'République du Cameroun' (The Republic of Cameroon) (Ngoh 1996).

The territory encompasses approximately 475.000sqkm, that is, 4/5 of the surface of France (Letouzey 1970). It is situated between 2°-13°N latitude, 9°-16° E longitude. Cameroon operates with two official languages – English and French, about 250 ethnic groups and about 270 local African languages and dialects, including pidgin. This gives it a culturally and geographically diversified nature which earned it the appellation 'Africa in Miniature' or 'the hinge of Africa'. It is headed by a President and a Prime Minister as the head of state and head of government respectively. The National Parliament constitutes 180 members with a speaker of the house. Cameroon operates a highly centralised system of administration dominated by the president. The country is broken down into administrative units of ten provinces, which are further broken into smaller units of divisions and subdivisions. Yaoundé is the capital city while Douala, which is the largest city and a metropolis, is the economic capital. The monetary unit is the CFA Franc.

The population as per the 2006 estimates stands at about 17,340,702 with an annual growth rate of 2% (2006). Birth is rated at 33.9/1000; infant mortality is rated at 63.5/1000; life expectancy stands at 51.2. Density per square mile is 96.

The climate of Cameroon varies with terrain, from tropical along the coasts to semiarid and hot in the north. The northern plains and the sahel region are semiarid and hot (seven month dry season); the central and western highlands where Yaounde is located is cooler, with shorter dry season; the southern tropical forest is warm with about four months dry season; the coastal tropical forest , where Douala is located is warm, humid throughout the year. The terrain is diverse. The south west constitutes the coastal plain; the centre is made up of dissected plateau; the west is mountainous while plains are in the north. The most active volcano in Cameroon, the Mount Fako is found in Buea, and is the highest elevation in the country. The main rivers are the Benue, Nyong and Sanaga. The land is used as follows: arable land

13% (as per the 2003 Agricultural Ministry estimate); permanent crops 2%; meadows and pastures constitute 18%; forest and woodland 54% and others 13%. Agriculture makes up 27% of GDP, manufacturing 30% of GDP, and Services 43% of the country's GDP.

The territory is rich in natural resources such as petroleum, bauxite, iron ore, timber, and hydro power potential, cobalt and nickel. Export products include crude oil and petroleum products, lumber, cocoa beans, aluminium, coffee, and cotton. Imports include machinery, electrical equipment, transport equipment, fuel and food. Current environmental problems facing Cameroon are the prevalence of water-borne diseases; deforestation, overgrazing, desertification, poaching, volcanic eruptions with release of poisonous gases. Thus, environmental degradation remains a major concern.

Education is compulsory between ages 6 and 14. The literacy rate is 75%. My study concerns part of the former British Cameroon - Buea.

Profile of Study area

Buea is a municipality that covers about twenty villages and serves as the administrative headquarters or capital of the South West Province, one of the ten provinces of Cameroon. It is a renowned town which served as the capital of Cameroon during German colonial era from 1901-1909, (Ngoh 1996). It also served as the capital of the United Nations (UN) Trust Territory of Southern Cameroons from 1919-1961. Prior to assuming the status of the administrative headquarters of the South West Province of Cameroon, it served as the headquarters of the Southern province of British Cameroons (1949-1961), and then as the capital of the seat of government of West Cameroon from 1961-1972, when the organisational structure of the country changed from a federal state to a unitary system of government. Buea hosts the University of Buea, the only Anglophone University in Cameroon. It still contains some traces of colonialism like some colonial buildings notably the palatial former residence of the German governor, Jesko Von Puttkamer. It is the only provincial capital in Cameroon that is a rural town. The other nine capitals are located in urban towns but Buea is a rural town because of its backwardness in socio-economic development, the most prominent being the absence of good markets; no good motor park; lack of farm to market roads.

Buea is located at the foot of Mount Cameroon (4095m) which is the highest mountain in West and Central Africa, and one of the most active volcanoes in Africa. It lies on the Eastern slopes of Mount Cameroon (which has erupted 7 times in the last century, most recently in June 2000). Buea constitutes a total of about 20 villages. The villages are spread out in a compact way with very thin lines or boundaries separating them. My study covers a selection of villages within this area. Some of the features that contrast Buea with the rest of the country are: Buea hosts the annual and famous Mount Cameroon race of hope. These attract many migrants and

tourists into the area. The presence of some colonial antiquities is an attractive point for many. It is a sub-division consisting of several villages; it represents the country's geographic and cultural diversity. In this regard, the ethnic composition of Buea is diverse. In addition to this, unlike other rural areas where the young people (the active and productive force of the land) migrate to the cities in search of jobs leaving behind only the old people and children, Buea booms with the most vibrant population who comprise students, unemployed graduates, and petty traders and so on.

Three kinds of governments operate in Buea namely the central government in the status of an appointed Divisional Officer (D.O); locally elected government – The Local Government (LG) called the Buea Rural Council (BRC); and lastly locally inherited government or native authorities – the chiefs. Each of these government forms has a function in Buea.[9] The LGs operating in Cameroon are City, Urban and Rural Councils depending on the level of development as well as population in each municipality. The BRC is headed by a Mayor, who is assisted by three deputies. This shall be given full coverage in a later chapter (chapter four) set aside for an overview of LGs.

Buea is also an area where many different political parties and political ideologies operate. Amongst them is the ruling party- the Cameroon Peoples Democratic Movement (CPDM); The Social Democratic Front (SDF), which is the most popular opposition party in Cameroon; The Union De Population Camerounaise (UPC); other small and unpopular parties and the most notable and radicalist Southern Cameroons National Council (SCNC). The SCNC is not a political party but is operating with a political ideology with the motive for the Anglophone Cameroonians (or English speaking Cameroonians) to secede and become an independent nation. This is precipitated by the fact that Anglophone Cameroonians are marginalised and their part of the country the least developed despite the fact that about 80% of the nation's natural resources are tapped from this area e.g. oil in Limbe, rubber, timber amongst others which form the basis of the nation's exporting industry.

Climate

Like the rest of the country, Buea enjoys a tropical climate with two distinct seasons: dry and rainy seasons. The rainy season lasts from around March to October, while the dry season lasts from November to February. The rainy season is marked by relatively low temperatures (about 15°C) during which moisture-laden and predominantly South-West Monsoon originate from the Atlantic Ocean and blow over the whole country. The peak of the rainy season falls between late June and early September when heavy downpours of tropical rain are experienced. On the other hand, the dry season is marked by abundant sunshine accompanied by high temperatures (about 30°C) especially during the day. Predominant winds during this season are the North-East trade winds (the Harmattans) which blow southwards from the Sahara desert into the country, bringing along dry conditions.

Because of its location at the foot of Mount Cameroon, Buea enjoys a considerably more temperate climate than the rest of the country which is generally cool but dry and humid, with maximum temperatures ranging between 25ºC and 33ºC. Humidity levels in the area often range between 75% and 80% during the months of November through February. Thunderstorms and damp fogs are common, rolling off the mountain into the city below.

Human and Economic Activities

Population

The population of Buea is estimated at 150.000 inhabitants as per the records of the last official census and covers a land mass or surface area of approximately 866km. Each village is headed by a chief who takes care of the

affairs of the village. Chieftaincy is a typical Cameroonian (and African) traditional structure. It is one of the oldest traditional institutions in Cameroon which has survived from pre-colonial, to colonial, to independence and post independence periods. They are known as traditional authorities. Administration during the colonial period incorporated traditional authorities whereby they were endorsed with specific roles such as collection of taxes and mobilization of communal labour. The independence and post independence periods saw the role of the chiefs limited to traditional and cultural matters as against the absolute control that chiefs had in matters of administration, judicial and political matters before the advent of colonization. The major activities of the chiefs today are carried out within the traditional council.

In Buea as well as most areas in Cameroon there exist a hierarchy of chiefs such that at the lowest level there is the village chief while at the highest level there is the paramount chief. Where there is a need for a project in the village, the chief assembles his elders in council who together deliberate on the matter and channel it to the council through an elected councillor under the council. There is a paramount chief (Chief Endeley) who is in charge of all the villages under Buea. He relates with the wider network. For example, when events such as trade fairs are organised, after consultation with the council he is the traditional head to be consulted to seek his permission for this to be effected. At the end of such a project the paramount chief, on behalf of the people of Buea gets a share of the proceeds, and the council gets a share. The original indigenes of Buea who constitute the majority of the population here are part of the indigenous people called the Bakweri whose native dialect is Mokpwe (Gordon

2005). Mokpwe is said to constitute part of the family of Duala languages in the Bantu group of the Niger-Congo language family. All the chiefs are Bakweri. Historically, the people of Buea are said to be closely related to Cameroon's coastal peoples (the Sawa) particularly the Dualas in the Central Province of Cameroon and the Isubu. Under the British and French colonial rule, they were split, one part (the Duala) falling under French

administration while the other (the Bakweri) fell under British administration. Due to its position as a university town since 1993, and the provincial capital, there are a significant number of people from other ethnic groups. Statistical data on the actual number of indigenes, migrants, and foreigners who inhabit in Buea is absent.

Land Tenure:

The 1992 Land Ordinance which was amended in 1996 states that all land is owned by the state and can be claimed at any time. This is with regard to the fact that the state has the right to appropriate for the imperative interest of the general public any parcel of land occupied by a private individual, group, family, a corporate body or any other entity. The imperative to do this may arise from interests such as the need for social and economic development and also national defence. Nonetheless, there is private ownership of land, and in such cases the owners of land acquired through legal procedures are compensated. Land can be owned through purchase or inheritance. Land can be bought through legal procedures from an individual with the interference of the state through state administrators like the S.D.O, and the D.O. In the event of any realization that developed land is found in a risky zone, it is automatically demolished though with compensation from the state for displacement. Land disputes are resolved by the D.O (who represents the state) upon invitation from the chief of the village. The same applies for land disputes that involve more villages except that in this case the invitation is from the paramount chief in the person of Chief E.M.L Endeley. In effect, land disputes are resolved by the law. In a case where villagers take upon themselves to bypass the chief and invite the D.O, the D.O still acknowledges the powers of the chief by consulting him before going ahead with the matter. The chief takes part in the settlement of land disputes because he is recognised by the state. Moreover, the land ordinance that gives the state ownership over all land is only applicable where the state has to embark on a project for the

benefit of all. And even at this, the chiefs must be consulted especially with regard to the fact that tradition plays a very important role in the African setting and in Buea particularly.

It should be noted that chiefs as custodians of land are recognised as partners in the management exercise. This is done with the assumption that resources are better managed when their local custodians have shared or exclusive rights to make decisions over and benefit from their use. In this regard, the chief representing his elders in council and village, has a right to disagree with the state over a piece of land from his village to be used especially if he feels it is not to the benefit of his people. Where he is not satisfied with the choice of the state, he can make a choice for them. However, in most cases it is the chief that is consulted and after deliberations with his people, allocates a piece of land for whatever purpose the state requires it.

Each chief has his own stretch of land and can from time to time declare use for certain pieces of communal land. This may either be for the protection of village property or for growing his personal food crops. Inheritance here is patrilineal where, upon the father's death, his property is split among his male children. When a villager who is the head of a family acquires land (where land is passed on through heritage) as a successor, he is then known as the occupant of the land on which he and his people settle and work. In the absence of the occupant of a piece of land, he can delegate someone to be in charge until his return. The chiefs are supposedly the embodiment of the values of their people.

Settlement

The houses are built close to each other in each village. This is to maintain easy communication with each other and ensure security and solidarity, a common feature of small communities where everyone knows everyone. Farmlands are about 1km far from the settlement area. The people have

traditionally practiced polygamy but with Christianisation which has gradually transformed the minds of the people especially after the 1970s, this custom has become extremely rare. Christians from different denominations are found in Buea like Roman Catholics and Protestants. Nevertheless, ancestor worship persists. They believe in the ancestors living in a parallel world and mediating for them (between the living and the gods). Their spirits inhabit the mountain and many of them believe that witchcraft holds a malign influence on everyday life. Traditional festivals held each year serve as the most visible expression of these traditional beliefs in modern times. Even in the most popular Mount Cameroon race of hope, rituals have to be performed on the mountain to appease the gods without which it is believed no one will come back alive. The chiefs represent a link with the past-the ancestors.

Economic Activities

The dominant economic activity in Buea is agriculture (about 80%) which forms the backbone of the local economy, and though agriculture in itself does not tell much about the level of development, we are apt to conclude here that the form of agriculture in Buea – which is characterised by low input/output and its subsistence oriented nature gives Buea a status of low socio-economic development. The people cultivate mainly food crops using rudimentary tools and depend on family labour. Their activities are more concentrated in the rainy season which marks the cultivation period while the dry season is for harvesting. The rainy reason is the busiest period in the lives of rural communities because agricultural production is predominantly rain-fed and the farming systems are particularly sensitive to small changes in climatic conditions. It is also the busiest period as it coincides with the longest academic vacation. This provides an opportunity for each household to increase its labour force with pupils and students most of whom have as a duty to labour for their tuition and school needs. In both the rainy and dry season women and children dominate in farm activities especially in labour supply. This reflects the sexual division of labour in Buea where the men actively take

part in clearing the bush while the women and children are left to do the rest such as burning, hoeing, weeding and harvesting. The farmers produce mainly maize, cassava, yams, cocoyam, plantains, potatoes and various kinds of vegetables. The farm products are usually for home consumption while the surplus is sold to the local markets and the income derived spent on other basic necessities.

Buea is void of forests. It is a savannah region. Owing to the location of the area which witnesses the deposition of volcanic and other related matter from the mountain, the soil in and around Buea is nutrient rich and provides high fertility for both natural vegetation and farmland. Hence, yields are healthy and abundant. The leaves of plants and trees here are far larger and the undergrowth particularly is richer. Though everything seems to grow at its best, the area is remarkable for its rocky nature which renders cultivation, building and road construction works difficult. Traders from other cities visit the local markets in Buea where they buy these farm produce very cheap and take to cities like Douala (the economic capital) where they sell at higher prices.

Apart from agriculture, the status of Buea as the provincial and municipal headquarter has made it possible for some of its inhabitants to hold administrative and other clerical positions in the formal sector. Some are employed at the Tole tea Estate which is part of the Cameroon Development Corporation (CDC), the second largest employer in Cameroon after the government; a significant number of public, mission and private primary and secondary schools, and government hospital alongside private clinics. This also brings many migrants into the area to work in these institutions. This increasing number of inhabitants triggers the need for more and improved services, that is, it should be accompanied by a corresponding increase and efficiency in infrastructural development as well as service delivery (social

facilities). The absence of such services commensurate to the population of Buea has subjected it to maintaining its status quo as a rural area.

Focus on the area of study gives the reader a fore knowledge and highlights of where this area is situated in Cameroon and the ecology, geography, geomorphology and history of these people. Elements such as their population, settlement patterns, land tenure, and economic activities have been examined. Agriculture forms the backbone of the economy of these people and women are more involved than the men. Buea is not only inhabited by the indigenes, it is the home of many people from different parts of Cameroon and also foreigners. Though modernity is fast having its roots in Buea, the people still hold firm some of their traditions which they believe are essential for their existence. Hence, the culture of the Buea people is very important in all spheres of life and even in designing and implementing policies.

Dynamism of Local Governments in Cameroon

Local Governments

Olowu et al (2004) conceives local governance as a rule-governed process through which residents of a defined area participate in governance in locally important matters; As key decision makers, they participate in determining their priority concerns, how to respond to them, the resources to realise these concerns; and in managing and learning from these responses. In this respect, representatives of local residents may and frequently perform these functions as agents of the people. They remain accountable to (and removable by) the people included in the local regime through specified procedures.

According to Law No 74-23 of 5 December 1974 organising councils in Cameroon, a 'rural council shall be a council whose territorial jurisdiction covers a built up area, with or without a town plan and rural areas whereas an urban council is a council whose territorial jurisdiction is confined to a built-up area having a town plan.'

Overview of Local Governments in Cameroon: A Historical Perspective
The Colonial Era

The period before 1961 was the colonial period in British Southern Cameroons. The area under study first witnessed German influence as the rest of the country and served as the capital of Cameroon during this period. It also witnessed British influence and control. Between 1922 and 1945, the

British implemented the policy of Indirect Rule thought to be the best rule in British Cameroon. During this period, the British created Native authorities through which they administered the people of British Cameroons (Finken 1996, Stark 1980).

The period 1945-1961 was characterised by nationalism. This period saw the formation of credit unions and political parties that fought for the independence of the territory though with different interests. Some parties wanted to attain independence by joining Nigeria; some wanted to achieve independence by joining French Cameroon; while others advocated secession without reunification. These were those who wanted British Cameroon to be an independent entity. An important element here is the fact that there was multiparty politics in Cameroon before independence. During this period the elites in British Cameroon took over from Native

Authorities. These elites were made up of sons of the soil who had attained a certain level of education mostly in the west (Europe or America). Local government areas were created and Buea fell under the Victoria Local Government. Chiefs had less influence as the power vested on them to manage their resources and affairs was transferred to local governments. The creation of Local Governments in Cameroon is to the credit of the colonial administration.

Post Colonial Era

Between 1961 and 1972 Cameroon was a Federation in a union between what became known as West Cameroon (British Cameroon) and East Cameroon (French Cameroon). Multiparty politics was abandoned in favour of one-party system to implement authoritarian rule which characterised this period in most young African states. Local Governments still existed but did not maintain a British style where LGs could exercise some authority over their people because the French believed they had annexed British Cameroon so they implemented French policies whereby the local elites had no say in any project that directly or indirectly affected their lives, thereby undermining

local Governments. In French Cameroon the colonial high commissioner supervised LGs because he insisted on having authority over them in order to keep the natives under control. This was transferred to the British part of Cameroon which institutionalized the decline in LG autonomy. The central government was the sole decision making body with the influence of the French who still had a grip on the country.

There was a tension between 1972 and 1990 in Cameroon. In 1972 a referendum was organised in which the people of Cameroon voted for a unitary state. A centralised government which ensued after the abolition of the federal system made Local governments' autonomy undermined. In 1974 councils were organised as LGs. Though they generated revenues through taxes basically, they could not utilise it directly because the figures were registered in the national treasury. In effect, they had no financial autonomy. The consequence of this tendency has been inadequate and inefficient development projects. Mayors were statutorily controlled by administrators (Senior Divisional Officers, SDOs) who are representatives of the state within local communities. Oyono (2004) notes that before the launching of political pluralism in 1990, the appointment of mayors was the common place.[10] Cognisance should be taken of the fact that the LGs that existed before 1974 covered very large areas of jurisdiction and Buea fell under the Victoria[11] LG area. In 1974 with the creation of councils, the areas of jurisdiction were narrowed down and Buea operated under the BRC. From 1990, the system was reformed with the institutionalization of democracy which has led to democratic decentralization and a supposed shift of power. In 1993 there was the first supposed democratic municipal election in Cameroon because of the reinstitution of multi-party politics in 1990. However, although declaring its interest in the strengthening of LG, the central state in fact controls them and

works towards their authoritarian deconstruction (Oyono 2004). The active role of S.D.Os and D.Os in this form of LG however highlights the limits and the instrumentality of this version of decentralization. The LG unit existing in Buea is the council called the Buea Rural Council.

The Organigram (Organisational Structure) of the BRC

Different political parties contest in the council elections and the party that is proclaimed victorious rules the council. The council is elected for a period of five years. After the party has been proclaimed victorious there is an internal election within the party to elect the councilors of the council. These councilors are elected based on their active participation in the party. When these councilors are elected they now vote within them the mayor and the deputies. How many terms a mayor stays in office are determined by his party (that is if the party keeps winning in elections) and how he works to impress the party. For the villages where the opposition wins the opposition presents one person who will act as a councilor for that village. It is important to note here that the party that wins in elections is very important when it comes to assessing the level of representativeness of the LG because over 90% of council workers belong to the same party except for those working on secondment who could belong to different parties and the few councilors from different parties. In villages where the opposition wins the party in question presents a councilor. But they are too few to have any influence on the decisions of the council. Implicitly, once the party in council is not a popular choice, the party cannot be a representative of the people.

The mayor is assisted by three deputies: first, second and third deputy mayors. They all have their functions to execute but in the absence of the mayor (in a case where he is out on duty), his duties are taken over by his deputies. Next to the deputy mayors is the Secretary General (SG) who is in

charge of council files and records. The Secretary General (SG) is a trained worker from the Local Government Training Centre- LGTC, commonly known by its French acronym CEFAM (Centre de Formation d'Administrative Municipal), appointed by the state. Directly under him is the Chief of Administration who is appointed by the mayor hence employed by the council. He therefore owes his allegiance to the mayor who must be satisfied with his work. The Finance Office keeps all financial records of the council. The financial treasurer is a trained civil servant of the state working on secondment to the council. There is a Health Unit for consultation of all those who find it convenient to come there. A Human Resource Unit is present. Their responsibility is to issue tickets to stores at the market and collect taxes. The Hygiene and Sanitation Unit is responsible for environmental cleanliness and aesthetics of the municipality. The councilors do not earn a monthly salary. They are only paid once in a while when they hold session meetings (ordinary sessions) which are convened by the mayor once every six months or extraordinary sessions when the need arises. This is because the councilors have other permanent jobs so they are not full time council workers. Each village councilor acts as an intermediary between his/her people and the council. Their roles can be summarized as follows: elect the mayor and his deputies; attend ordinary and extraordinary council sessions; vote the council budget and approve administrative accounts; grant special revenue and expenditure authorizations; contract loans and accept gifts and legacies; authorize council intervention in the economic and social spheres; approve town plans (names for streets, public squares and places);authorize the purchase of real estate, authorize the holding and abolition of fairs, and authorize the cession or exchange of council property.

The Processes of Decision Making at the Council

This section examines how the council as an elected body relates with the chiefs as traditional authorities and then with the state. It looks into the processes of power relations, that is, who defines what and who are the beneficiaries? This will provide a foundation to evaluate whether there is decentralization and if this has led to empowerment or not and who partakes in decision making.

The Council and the Chiefs

There is a line between the functions of the council and those of the chiefs. Their functions are parallel in a way. Issues related to socio-economic development and politics are handled by the council. For example, during a Minister's official visit, he is welcome by the mayor of the town. In the event of a football match or a trade fair, money is paid in to the council for using council property (the stadium and the town ground) in Buea. Here the chiefs have no role to play except the paramount chief whose presence may be imperative for the pouring of libation.[12] This is most important in the Mount Cameroon race where the gods of the mountain must be appeased else no one dares to climb the mountain because it will result to death. The chiefs are custodians of tradition in their villages and so take care of all matters strictly related to that. Projects to be executed by the council around the municipality can be determined by the Lord Mayor who has the power to single-handedly take the final decision depending on the budget at hand. At the beginning of each year, the socio-economic problems of each village are channeled to the council by each councilor. The mayor then summons a session where deliberations are made and final decisions taken as to which projects are to be

carried out that year and in what preference. The mayor also has executive rights to decide what to do in such cases.

The chiefs in turn are answerable to the paramount chief who acts as the general overseer of all traditional matters such as death rites, pouring of libation, and so on. Where such matters are above a chief in his village they are channeled to the paramount chief.

The Council and the State

The state exercises control over the council through its supervisory authorities-the Divisional Office(r) or Senior Divisional Office(r); the second level of supervisory authority is the governor who is in charge of the whole province; then the Minister of Territorial Administration and Decentralization; the Prime Minister, and finally the President. All these administrators except the president are appointed. They all have supervisory powers at different levels but I concentrate on the S.D.O because it is the immediate supervisory authority operating at the same level with the council. The state implements working methods which are assumed to be capable of improving the efficiency and quality of council services. The S.D.O is placed in an office with subordinates. The S.D.O visas resolutions of the council; approves municipal orders; checks council accounts; can take the place of the mayor; rectifies council budget; approves the delegation of power from mayor to deputies, and can draw up a budget in case of failure of the council executive. The council is therefore accountable to the state because the state still has control and therefore defines council powers and duties. The S.D.O also ensures the maintenance of peace and order in the council area and the division. He/she coordinates activities of various government services and attends council sessions.

CEFAM

We cannot talk about the LG in Cameroon without mentioning CEFAM (Centre de Formation d'Administrative Municipal – LGTC – Local Government Training Centre). CEFAM is a public establishment placed under the responsibility of a director, with legal personality and financial autonomy. Its function is to train LG workers. The aim is to provide training, further training, and refresher courses for the administrative and technical staff of councils, council unions and council establishments: the personnel with supervisory powers over councils and the personnel of the civil status registries. They organize on-site and off-site training programmes, colloquiums, seminars, workshops and conferences on all council affairs.

The Role of the Buea Rural Council in the Transformation of Buea:

The role of the council, as stated by the law organising councils is to administer local affairs to secure the economic, social and cultural development of its population. In this respect, LGs play a major role in the effort to create conditions for sustainable development and poverty reduction by ensuring more effective and accountable local infrastructure and service delivery for the poor and by improving dialogue between the state, citizens and their communities and the private sector. This is facilitated through their various activities under different projects which have been creating multiple long term and short term employment opportunities for the poverty stricken people.

Between 1993 and 2003, the Buea Rural Council (BRC) has recorded some achievements. Some of the projects carried out include:

Transport

Land transport, being the only means of transport here, is highly influenced by nature. The road network that is almost inaccessible makes movement difficult. This is caused by the muddy nature of the untarred roads in the rainy season. In some cases there are only footpaths linking one village to another. The BRC has constructed some bridges to link up villages, numerous concrete culverts, construction of some taxi bays, tarring of some roads, construction of a car park at the council and a general motor park for inter and intra-town transport. The construction of some of these roads has facilitated the movement of people and farm produce to other markets where the produce are sold higher, thus bringing in revenue for the local people who can embark on other investments.

Markets

Apart from constructing other small markets in the villages, the main market which is located in Buea town has been given some attention with the construction of a bigger market and a slaughter house, construction of meat slap, construction of model stalls (the construction is still in progress). This market, held on a daily basis, attracts people from far and wide to come and buy or sell. Apart from the Buea town market and the Muea market that are witnessing the construction of some stores, all the other markets in this municipality are open aired and this renders it difficult for people to buy and sell. In the rainy season the rain is a problem and in the dry season the sun too is overbearing. Nonetheless, the dry season is better than the rainy season. The markets in the Buea municipality attract people from other towns who come to

buy mostly foodstuff at cheaper rates to go and sell. But since the roads are not good enough the Muea market, which is along the main road linking Buea with other towns has an advantage over the other markets.

The villages all have different market days where they buy and sell their products. These markets are held weekly while some other markets like the Muea market holds twice a week. The Buea Town market which is the biggest market is held daily.

Health

The health post at Bova (one of the villages) which was almost out of use has been renovated so that the people do not have to travel long distances to seek for health services for minor cases. A laboratory has also been constructed at the Buea

Town health centre. Not all the villages in this municipality have

health centres so the people have to travel long distances to seek medical care. In effect, the population is more than can be handled and this renders health services poor. Though some few promising and relatively efficient private health centres do operate in some of the villages like Bunduma, these are too expensive for the pockets of the rural folk

Schools and Community Development Projects

For many schools that existed without complete buildings and efficient teachers, benches, roofing sheets were donated or provided including some teachers under the financial support of the BRC for effective and efficient learning. There is at least a public school in each village in Buea. Every child has access to school but most parents can only afford primary education which is the level where the children attain their First School Leaving Certificate (FSLC). Primary school has seven classes – class one to class seven- at the end of which the final exam is taken into secondary school. After this level some parents send their children to secondary school either private for those who can afford or public. They may choose to send the children to secondary schools in Buea or out of Buea. Some parents send their children to learn trades such as mechanic, driving, tailoring, hairdressing, while still some leave the children at home to help in farm work or do hocking.

Some other projects realized include the renovation of Staff Quarters at Buea and Muea, construction of public toilet at Buea town, conversion of old slaughter house Buea town into office facilities, renovation and extension of Secretary General's residence, maintenance of the BRC hall/compound, Construction of Bokoko-Woloko-

Molyko Water Supply (a project funded by the British High Commission), and improvement of water supply to Muea (one of the villages), amongst others.

As mentioned before, Buea has one of the purest sources of water in Cameroon. There are few public taps to provide water for household consumption. This water is free for all. In Molyko, which is the university students' residential area, most houses that are constructed have water connection so that the students don't have to go out to fetch water. But the students have to pay monthly bills for their consumption.

Other Projects

Because of the concern for the environment and human life, a demolition project was carried out where houses built in risk zones were demolished. Still in connection with this, shades for business as well as calaboat houses (houses built with wood) for private residence built along the road that rendered the town dirty and unattractive were demolished. This has given way to the construction of good structures along road.

It should be noted that some of these projects are still in their premature state till date, while still others are incomplete. The reasons for this revolve around the Local Government institution which has shifted from being a development driver to a party unit. This will be further discussed in chapter five.

Employment

The BRC offers long and short term employment opportunities to the Buea folk. Long term job offers concern those that are given on permanent basis to the people in this municipality while short term jobs are granted to students on vacation to earn money that can help in one way or the other to provide their school needs when school resumes. Short term jobs are also provided on contract basis to those working on council projects. Moreover, municipal workers change when power changes hands. This implies that while some people get employed, others are bound to lose their jobs.

Generation of Funds

For the council to operate, it requires funds. So, how does the council raise funds for its functioning? There are many ways that the BRC raises funds to carry out its activities. The council depends mainly on local taxes that are collected from the market through market tolls. Other sources include: revenue from hocker licences, lease of the town hall and other council property such as the trucks, payment from the use of the stadium during football matches and other activities such as the Mount Cameroon Race of Hope and Trade Fairs. They also raise funds from civil status registry such as Birth Certificates and Marriage

Certificates; advertisement fees – to put up a barner or bill board in the municipality you have to pay a quarter to the council. The law also demands that the council makes money from building permits. For a structure to be put up, the council has to be consulted through an application, whereby

the council will send council technicians to inspect the area to ascertain the suitability of the structure and then levy a small fee.

The council is also subsidized by FEICOM (Special Council Support Fund). FEICOM is a government institution with a mission to assist councils realize council projects like roads, water and electricity. This support can be financial or material. This institution gets its funding from money generated by councils. This is an indication that councils raise enough funds to be self- sufficient.

It is also the responsibility of the council to create national and international contacts where they can solicit aid. It could be from development agencies, associations or even governments. This aid is granted in most cases on condition that a project is on the pipeline.

These projects will act as a yardstick for assessing the performance of the Buea Rural Council. The identification of projects is a process that involves the local people and the LG. The chief of each village and his elders in council sit and discuss the needs of the village. These needs are channelled to the LG through the councilors representing each village.

This section has given us a historical overview of LGs in Cameroon. LGs existed since colonial times till after independence which indicates that decentralization is not a new phenomenon in Cameroon but it has existed in different dimensions. Throughout the existence of LGs, mayors were appointed until after 1990 when democratic decentralization was set in place. Also discussed here are the structure and functioning of the BRC and how the BRC relates with the state, the traditional authorities and the ordinary people. It also identifies some projects carried out by the BRC in their municipality and this will lay the groundwork for the assessment of their performance. This reflection on the overview of LGs in Cameroon will be used to support some components of the arguments in the analysis, which is concerned with the

holding back and taking over of democratic decentralization in efforts towards development, a practice generated and reproduced by the central state's representatives and officials.

Facts Interpretation

In this chapter, data is analysed based on how the different actors involved in the development process in Buea perceive the outcome. Since the transformation involves an interface of actors, the perception of the impact varies according to the actors involved, in this case the ordinary people and the Buea Rural Council (BRC) officials (both elected and appointed). Within the council it varies especially with regard to political ideologies reflecting different political parties. Party views constitute an important element in the analysis considering the fact that two different parties have headed the BRC within the period under study. Hence, the analysis will adopt a critical approach. As previously mentioned, Buea is an expanding town population wise. This population expansion is supposed to be accompanied by a corresponding increase in economic activities and social services, which are commensurate with the needs of the people. Measuring the progress of Buea is made by comparing it with other cases such as the other 9 headquarters – Yaounde for the Centre province; Douala for Littoral province; Maroua for the Far North province; Garoua for the North province; Ngoundere for the Adamawa province; Bafoussam for the West province; Ebolowa for the South province and Bertoua for the East province - and the progress of Cameroon to other West and Central African states. This is based on the contention that we never see the true state of our condition until it is illustrated to us by its contraries, neither can we really value what we enjoy, except by the want of it. An assessment of the projects will serve as a point of departure in this analysis.

Performance of the Buea Rural Council:
An Appraisal/Assessment of Council Projects from Actors' Perspectives
BRC Perspective

With party interests aside, the councils are governmental institutions with standards within which they operate and those standards have no party connotation. But there might be party interests when it comes to evaluating and even looking at the practical application of those standards. The government officials (auditors of the council) may choose to be more scrupulous with an opposing party and less scrupulous with the government party so there are differences in the evaluation and application of what councils are supposed to do. The basic is that councils are run within a regulation because there was the law of 1974 which was the law being utilized. From time to time there are decrees and amendments to suit the government's intention to decentralize.

According to the BRC representatives, they have recorded some remarkable successes in relation to the available resources. Most of the successes they enumerated are infrastructural such as the construction of culverts and bridges. The most notable development that has taken place according to them is the provision of pipe-borne water especially in Molyko which has access to public taps. Molyko is mostly a student residential area. This has reduced the inconveniences of walking long distances to fetch water. It should be noted that Buea has one of the purest sources of water in Cameroon. Travellers enjoy stopping over to fetch water and take away to their towns. However, not everybody within the council agrees on this.

It is expedient to place the BRC within party contexts to be able to clearly unravel the mysteries behind the scene. It is also important to place it within party contexts because the party that heads the council automatically

becomes the owner with almost all the workers belonging to that party. When there is a change in government at the council where representatives change, there is also a change in workers. This means that people lose their jobs when power changes hands.

Party Views

Before going into the perceptions of the different political parties that have run the BRC within the period under study, it is important to give a brief and concrete picture of the party structure at both national and local contexts for a fuller understanding of the situation at hand. The two most prominent political parties in Buea, the

Cameroon Peoples' Democratic Movement (CPDM) and the Social Democratic Front (SDF) hold different views as to the performance of the LG and these different views are presented. There are other political parties operating in Buea but they are not popular. The CPDM and SDF are the two parties that have headed the BRC within the period under study and I thought it was pertinent to talk to both mayors. The CPDM party is the party in power at national level and its headquarters is in the nations' capital, Yaounde. It is the ruling political party in Cameroon, which evolved from an earlier political party in 1985, the Cameroon National Union (CNU) that had dominated Cameroon politics since independence. The objectives and policies have remained the same. When this new political party was created, many political analysts were of the opinion that a new political era had downed in Cameroon. The party's goals include: the fervent wish to get all on board through a New Deal; a new vision of militancy; a resolve towards national integration as the basis of peace, stability and prosperity. This party has been authoritarian in its activities until 1990 when democracy was reintroduced. However, even with the liberalization of the political landscape, the situation has not changed especially as their party ideologies seem quite different from what they do in practice.

On the other hand, the SDF is the most popular national opposition party in Cameroon that was created in 1990 when multiparty politics was reintroduced. The SDF party has never been in power at the national level. Since the launching of the party in 1990, they have led a series of non-violent crusades propagating democracy, respect for human rights and social justice in Cameroon. With their motto: Power to the people and Equal Opportunity, they promise to offer much to the people. The headquarters is in the North West Province capital, Bamenda. In accordance with its manifesto and constitution of 1990, the SDF pledges what can be summarised as follows: Uphold true national unity as the most appropriate political environment for real development; mobilize Cameroonians to establish a just, free and democratic society where everyone can live in dignity; guarantee freedom under the law and the respect for individual fundamental human rights; abolish all forms of oppression and suppression; adopt participatory democracy and government as the best means of getting every citizen involved in the political and development process; pursue a policy of winning power through elections; devolution of powers; and also uphold human dignity and the right to pursue lawfully and freely, ends which maximise and sustain individual group and societal happiness. These are their ideologies, and for the councils they have headed, they have tried to put these ideologies into practice. No body can predict whether the situation would change should they win at national level. What is important is what they have done so far.

The SDF Party in Council

The Social Democratic Front (SDF) party headed the BRC from 1996-1999. The SDF militants and popular opinion admitted that during this period the council was representative of the peoples' wishes and aspirations. There was a groundswell, and the vote difference showed that it was a significant victory. It should be noted that for an opposition party to be proclaimed victorious in any area in Cameroon is an indication that the party is very popular because the government has every machinery (financial and administrative powers especially) at its disposal to default elections. However, in this particular case the state underestimated the popularity of the party until the results were proclaimed. That accounts for why the state did everything possible to make sure the SDF did not head the council for a second term. If elections are free and fair, this is the party that will win in Buea over and over again first because of its popularity (which stems from the values they are advocating- power to the people and equal opportunity) and secondly because they worked according to the aspirations of the people, that is, they complied with their ideologies and promises.

The S.D.F admitted that for the period they headed the council, the frequency of supervision and audits was high in order to suppress representatives and cause the party to register failures and lose popularity. The then mayor made it clear that at certain points in time he had to flaunt the law to satisfy the people he was representing. A practical example he gave was in the execution of projects. The mayor is not authorized, according to the law, to sign for a project costing more than 10million francs CFA. This is how the delays come because the mayor has to procure the signature of the immediate supervisory authority. It may be a very meaningful project for the community, but he is forced to go through administrative bottlenecks to procure this signature. He did go around the law to execute projects for 20 million francs CFA and even more. Such projects include the construction of the Muea market. What was done to curb this lengthy procedure was to piece the projects up into bits of 5million francs CFA which he could sign. Each project has phases so he pieced them up into these phases and signed at each phase as long as he felt it was within his competence and he was able to do something for the people. He was questioned and had problems with the central government authorities. However this would not have affected him had elections been free and fair because he still remained the choice of the people. This situation presents empowerment of the people (he was their choice), and points to the fact that if the LG is completely empowered, Buea will be

transformed within a very short time. He took power upon himself and with the support of the ordinary people he realized much more than the other party. Implicitly, he was more flexible.

Reference was also made to the fact that when the representative is the choice of the people, many benefits accrue. For example, for most of the projects carried out during the SDF term of office, they spent less than what had been anticipated. Depending on their disposition, the local people were always willing to put in their best so they would come together with their talents and do a job faster and cheaper than in a case where another person is paid to do it. For example, if a culvert is to be constructed, many builders will put in their man power and if they are to be paid they demand less as they will also benefit from that.

The CPDM Party in Council

Though majority of the Buea Rural Council (BRC) officials of the CPDM party which is now heading the council share a common vision as to the achievements of the council (majority seemed unanimous), some critical voices were recorded. This is the ruling party at national level so it has national support. It was found out that within the party there was conflict as to the choice of the mayor. Popular opinion admitted this and it was confirmed by a female councillor of the CPDM regime, who said,

> The ascendancy of the mayor brought a lot of problems in the council. Sometimes the mayor delegates power to his deputy to represent him somewhere and the deputy categorically refuses (because of lack of cooperation and some of them are disgruntled with the mayor's input which will intend affect all of them). When a law is voted by the councillors it fails to be effected. The Lord Mayor uses his executive rights to do what he wants. The greatest good for the greatest majority is not respected but he does the greatest good for a very few people. You see council trucks transporting wood for the mayor's friends and close pals while full trash cans lie around town. Moreover, the trucks are fuelled by the
>
> council so it is a waste of council resources. These are some of the things that retard development. We can

count very little achievements which cannot really be felt by the people because the people are really in need.

This councillor feels they will have nothing to tell the local people should they contest for another term because they have failed in their expectations. From her perspective it can be deduced that the council is not representative of the people. Most of the workers at the BRC relied on the election results to say that the council is representative of the people but they refuse to admit the true nature of these elections. The CPDM however works with the authorities since they are 'players in the same team' (or belong to the same party). When asked how they reconcile the needs of the people and the provisions of the law, the answer was that the law takes precedence and that their activities must be bound by the law.

The Local People Speak

According to the information recorded from the ordinary people who include indigenes of Buea and permanent residents, the BRC has recorded some achievements but which are far below expectation. The people feel that the LG is not efficient. Resources intended for the transformation of this municipality are mismanaged and stolen by some unscrupulous workers who, because they belong to the so called "national team" are not questioned. It is also evident that Buea is not receiving the kind of sustained attention it merits from the BRC because the council is not answerable to them, but to the state. For example, if the representative is accountable to the local people, it gives the people the right to cast a vote of non-confidence when they are not satisfied with his achievements. That is not the case in Buea and Cameroon. Moreover, the council does not operate as a system (or public institution) but as a party. When asked what they think the council can do to improve on their situation, they mentioned they need more taps, road maintenance and construction of

markets. Above all, they mentioned that their involvement in decision making was crucial.

Talking about the general situation of the environment, they frowned at the piles of garbage in and around Buea. The BRC has placed trashcans in some points in Buea, yet, these cans overflow with rubbish and are not emptied. Worse still, the trashcans are too few and too small for the population. When they are full, inhabitants dump their rubbish beside them. One respondent said it was because of lack of cooperation, coordination and negotiation between the BRC and the local people. The situation is made worse by the town's poor drainage system. During the rainy season, runoffs invade the major streets impeding the traffic. The drainage system in some places gets blocked by rubbish, diverting runoffs into homes, which adversely affects the environment and poses a health threat. To illustrate the level of socio-economic backwardness of Buea, a retired Buea native who has spent most of his years out of the country working with the UNO and other international organizations made this remark,

> I grew up here as a little child and went to the Buea town market. I am now getting old and seeing the same market. The market cannot continue to be like that. Every Tuesday and Saturday (which are Buea town market days), there is an eye sore in Great Soppo as people crisscross the boulevard to do their shopping. Is that really befitting of a place which was the first capital of Cameroon? And there are places in Buea which could be better planned if one could have access to roads.

This shows how disgruntled the people are with the situation of the area and their disappointment with the BRC. He represents the views of the educated as well as the common villagers. Respondents also attested to the fact that when the SDF was in power (as the popular choice), much was achieved, that is, they confirm that about 85% of the achievements recorded by the BRC are projects that the SDF executed (completed projects). This gives the impression

that with the choice of the people, Buea can attain a satisfactory level of change.

The issue of devolution of power is still a myth yet to become reality. This has to do first with the question of the wrong party in power which is not the choice of the people, and secondly the indisputable grip of the state on councils. The question of empowerment was put to them in different ways that were easier for them to understand. Words such as rights, freedom were interchangeably used and they had a good understanding of these. From this, one can draw the conclusion that the people are far from being empowered based on their statements. Much success could be registered within the ten years under study with the metamorphosis of governance, they contend, but empowerment, a catalyst for development, is still absent and there is dire need for it. The local people identified certain problems that they were concerned with such as incomplete projects, no priority to projects, spreading thinly out, and no genuine representation of the BRC. One of the biggest problems the people identified is the nature of elections as a yardstick for representation.

Prioritization of Projects

Prioritizing projects is a good mechanism especially when council resources are limited, and where it is difficult to satisfy everyone at the same time. But the criteria for doing this are what the people do not understand. One project is as important to one village as another is important to another village. Therefore, negotiation is necessary. The people complain that with the CPDM in council things are quite different. Any village noted to have cast many votes for the opposition party is relegated to the background and most projects are carried out based on who is the closest friend of the mayor and his close collaborators (this concerns the present mayor). Moreover, government has almost made it a policy that dictates that anything that does not serve the personal or collective interest of those in power does not matter. That is why

the ruling national party seems to have almost made it a policy that those who vote against it are enemies of the state and are therefore treated accordingly.

With respect to the prioritization of projects, genuine representation exists only where there are such controls – accountability to the represented. The point of holding him/her to account after he acts is to make him/her act in a certain way – look after his constituents and do what they want, by reaching a negotiation where there is a disagreement. Accountability theorists assert that one is held responsible in order that he may become responsible, that is, responsive to the needs, and claims of those under him, to the obligations implicit in his position (Pitkin 1967). What exists in Buea instead is something concordant with the authoritarian view, which gives the state authority and new rights but places no obligation or control on them.

Incomplete Works

Some of the problems of the BRC are made worse by incomplete works. For example, respondents complained that some holes that were dug for some constructions have automatically been turned into rubbish dumps because they were abandoned. Moreover, "if the council claims that resources are limited, why go in for many projects at a time and end up not completing any?" one respondent wondered aloud. If they want to start with the Muea market (Muea is one of the villages in the municipality), they should finish up with the market. But we see here they start with the Muea market and the Mile 17 motor park at the same time. If at all they manage to finish one, it would have taken years such that by the time it is completed, some of the early parts are already ruined and need to be reconstructed. But with no money, it would be left like that, yet, they will claim that they have done this or that. The Muea market that was under construction is still uncompleted and other projects have come up.

Representativeness of the BRC
1: Table showing what respondents think about the representativeness of the BRC

	Average Frequency (AF)	Relative Frequency (RF%)
Representative	37	34.26
Not representative	66	61.11

Don't Know	5	4.63
Total	108	100

Majority of the respondents (61%) admitted that the BRC does not depict a true representative, while 34.26% thought the council is representative. The reasons the respondents gave were all directed to the nature of elections. There was a general cry of election malpractices and in their opinion, the SDF was the party that was supposed to win had elections been free and fair. This is an indication of the popularity of the opposition in this area and the general nature of elections in the country. If the representatives are not the choice of the electorate, there is no reason it should be termed a representative and there is no way the people can be said to be empowered when their rights are not respected. In such a situation, the representatives have no responsibility for accountability to their electorate because their allegiance goes to those at the top who hold the manipulative tools to put them in power. Accountability is introduced as a response and a corrective to authoritarianism. The distinguishing features of a representative government include genuine elections, a real choice of candidates, and free communications.

The Nature of Elections

The level of representativeness of the LG is dependent or largely determined by elections. Where elections are free and fair, the LG is representative because then it represents a majority. But where elections are dominated by malpractices, then the LG ceases to be the peoples' representative. In this case, it represents only a small sector of the population, i.e, a minority.), and the voices of the people are not heard. The people admitted that finding it hard to win free and fair elections in the new multiparty system, the ruling government has tried to perpetuate itself in power by using foul means to win elections. Elections are flawed with numerous irregularities such as the exclusion of a substantial proportion of the voting population from the voting exercise restraining participation in elections where all those who are eligible are unable to vote. This happens in different ways: Campaign strategies revolve around maintaining a high degree of political ignorance among the electorate; Most of the electorate are denied their voting rights especially in cases where their names fail to appear on the voters' register and this has led to strike action from the youth on several occasions. It should however be noted that not everyone of voting age registers to vote (and this cannot be blamed on anyone), but all registered voters should be accorded the right to choose their representatives. Some who register never find their names on the voting lists and would only be informed after the elections that their names appeared on lists in different constituencies. Worse still, names of people who are long dead appear on the voting lists. How then can we say the council is representative of the people when elections are characterised by malpractices. As is the general case with Cameroon, the local people confirmed that the last municipal elections in Buea were rigged because according to them, if elections were free and fair, the SDF party is to be the party in council.

At the level of the state and the LG, the people are of the opinion that the LG lacks the autonomy it deserves to effectively respond to its expectations. The success of the work of the BRC is restrained by the kinds of

functions and resources that have been devolved to them. They neither have financial, political, nor administrative autonomy.

According to the local people, there is power struggle within the LG. Buea is the casualty of such a struggle. It is usually said that "when two elephants fight, the grass suffer". This power struggle is consequential to the development of Buea. Only by putting aside these differences, can progress be realised. The development of Buea should be a common goal that should unit all actors concerned to be fully committed. Asked how the LG operates, most respondents contended that some people and LG administrators in this case, do not understand fully well the meaning of development. The task of developing Buea should be the priority of everyone in the community, in which case, party interests should not constitute an obstacle to commitment. The LG representatives are more concerned with their political interests (appointments to higher positions of government) than the transformation of Buea.

According to Janda (2005) a democracy needs strong and sustainable political parties with the capacity to represent citizens and provide policy choices that demonstrate their ability to govern for the public good. This is not the case of Cameroon where the ruling party uses state machinery in their own favour (for example, respondents quoted cases where the ruling party pays university students and hire buses that takes these students to rural areas to vote from one poling station to the other swelling the number of votes for the CPDM party). This is perceived as a major threat to the operation of strong political parties as well as a threat to free and fair elections. It is also a mechanism to weaken other political parties. Data from the field revealed that the C.P.D.M party, which is not so popular in Buea struggle for power through what can be termed 'democratic deficit'. The sequence of events after the elections that saw the CPDM heading the BRC revealed that elections were defaulted. This fraud was carried out with the support of the central

government and it happened in the whole nation. The local people said though the central government always expresses a verbal concern to redress this issue, nothing is done to curb the situation.

How Elections are rigged

There are rules and regulations binding the electoral system. The moment these rules and regulations are defaulted, then rigging machinery has already been set aground. The regulations state that the list of voters should be published for a period before the elections, when this voters' list fails to be published, it is an indication of an intention to rig. If on establishing the voters' register and in the course of distribution the voter centre is dislocated, it is an aspect of rigging. Dislocating a voter's centre means a voter registers in Buea, but his/her name fails to appear in the voters' register in Buea. Instead it appears in another area far from Buea where he will only find out after the elections thus hindering him/her from voting. When the administration engages bullies to harass people at voting centres it is an aspect of rigging. The use of ambulance voters, that is, people you carry from one point to the other to vote and swell the number of votes; If in the course of reviving the electoral register the names of people who were long dead are brought to light, and people who are not living in Buea are registered under Buea, all these constitute rigging.

Women Empowerment

Women said that they do not partake in the deliberations pertaining to the identification of projects. In the villages the identification of project is done by the chiefs and the elders in council who are all males. This is a typical tradition common in the whole country where it is believed that the fate of the community is in the hands of the men so women don't take part in village

councils. But at the LG level where there is a possibility of women standing as councilors (this is largely dependent on their political commitment), women partake in deliberations. In the BRC, the third assistant mayor is a woman and a few female councillors. This does not really portray a democratic system and empowerment of the woman because women are under-represented in decision making and the development of Buea. Though men were more represented than women, women saw things in the same direction as men. Both acknowledge the efforts which the BRC is making but were of the opinion that it was inadequate and inefficient.

The rural women in Buea enumerated their problems which range from the lack of capital, social amenities such as electricity, health, poor education, communication, and infrastructure. As managers of the home, and as the most vulnerable together with the children, they identified health services as their prime concern. They frown at the long distances they had to travel to secure their health and that of their children.

General Discussion on the Performance of the Buea Rural Council

The above findings are discussed in relation to some studies. From the findings, and from the perspectives of the various actors involved, it can be said that the Buea Rural Council (BRC) has recorded some achievements within the period under study. This reveals that the process of decentralization is actually in place because the local people participate in the identification of projects which implies that they take part in decision making though in a limited way. The projects that have been carried out so far are in response to the needs of the people such as the construction of markets, roads, culverts, renovation of health centre, provision of pipe-borne water and others, but these needs are not responded to in a satisfactory way. Therefore, in spite of the participation of the local people which has been made possible through

decentralization, the people are of the opinion that the state still maintains its dominant position over decision making through its supervisory agents that is, indicating the supremacy of the state over the councils. The claim that power has been devolved in Cameroon is questionable. Ideologically, yes, but the practical implementation and evaluation are quite different from the universal context and standards.

Elected councils are established to promote and ensure a bottom-up representation but surprisingly, it turns out to be a top-down execution of developmental intervention, initiated by the state, accompanied by strict surveillance.

The question then is 'what about the electorate, those who are the direct recipients of such duties, those who bear the consequences of all actions imposed to the council by the state? This does not reflect a shift of power. The law states that a municipal council can be dissolved by decree in which case the supervisory authority appoints a special commission of seven persons inclusive of the chairman and vice to head the council. Unfortunately the local people are not given the power to cast a vote of non confidence to the mayor for this to happen. The state takes upon itself through its personal assessment by its supervisory agents, to implement such an act. Is this a democratic act, because Shaw (2004) posits that when state involvement is less, there is a guarantee of more democracy. For an appointed administrator to supervise an elected administrator is not a measure suitable for participation and does not project a democratic principle. It would make sense for the state to send appraisers or evaluators to look critically at a project they are funding or to evaluate the democratic performance at local level. However, it cannot be the case because these are players belonging to the same team, playing what we could term 'politics of the stomach'.

Some projects started by one regime were abandoned by the council which were already at the level of completion before power changed hands. The new mayor abandoned these projects because they were initiated and

started by another regime. The question is: Is the BRC operating according to party, or is it working as the BRC for the common good of all? The logic is that whichever party rules and goes but the BRC remains. So why put party interests above peoples' welfare? As soon as power changes hands, the new representatives start all over again depicting a discontinuity. Though the council operates as an institution, the situation of these two prominent political parties is presented to buttress the fact that with empowerment comes more progress and achievements. It was earlier noted that most of the achievements recorded by the BRC were put in place by the SDF party which is the strongest and most popular opposition party in the country.

With regard to representation, there is the problem of the wrong party in the council which makes the LG unrepresentative. Quoting Pogge (2002) Banik argues if there is any reason to tell [the ruled] that their leaders are to blame or that the global community is unfair for the persistence of poverty and other related problems which they are facing. He goes ahead to ask this question, "What then do we do when the [ruled] respond by saying that they did not choose their leaders in the first place?" (Banik 2006). This is a big challenge looking at the case of Buea, where a majority of respondents say the party in council is not the choice of the people because elections were rigged.

The whole ideology of democracy and decentralization exist, but not in practice which implies it is not full flesh decentralization. With respect to democracy, it is a democratic process in a sense because there are certain elements of democracy such as the organisation of elections but the nature of elections lacks democratic ideals. In effect, there is decentralization without empowerment. Hence, the state and the representatives are criticized for their frequent shifts in concerns and policies that reflect the needs of the local people. Webster (1990) accounts for the limitation of the ability of LG institutions to provide 'voice' to the local populace to their role as, for the most part, implementers of government programmes rather than instigators of development in their own right. Centralization of power (non-devolution) is

therefore the major explanation for the persistence of the low socio-economic profile of Buea. For this reason there is inadequate participation of the people and low level of commitment.

Though the BRC authorities blame their inability to respond adequately and efficiently to the needs of the people on the lack of resources, I explain this largely to lack of autonomy of the council. Looking at it from an objective perspective, the BRC raises funds to run the council but these funds are not controlled by the BRC. Another institution (FEICOM) is put in place to manage these funds which gives them the power to scrutinise and decide when and how to sign funds for the council. The situation presented of this institution (FEICOM) by the ordinary people and the BRC authorities of the different regimes is one of mismanagement and discrimination. FEICOM is used as another control mechanism on councils that are not pro-government runned. Such councils are denied assistance from FEICOM to make sure that they achieve very little to the dissatisfaction of the people under its constituent so that the people will lose trust in that particular party and then turn to the ruling party. The question that comes to mind here is, "if councils are capable of raising funds, why channel these funds to another institution which has to control the funds? Is the state not creating more and more avenues for embezzlement and corruption? Is the state not creating avenues to slow down development in minority groups? For example, the council complained that for the past four years councils in the Anglophone parts of Cameroon (the North West and South West Provinces) have not benefited any subventions from FEICOM. This was attributed to embezzlement of funds by the director of the institution who just happened to be sacked and a new director appointed. My opinion is that if FEICOM is not funded by the state to give subventions to councils then it has no reason to exist.

Constraints on Empowerment

The results of the study demonstrate that some factors are accountable for the inability of the Local Government (LG) to respond adequately and efficiently to the aspirations of the people of Buea and Cameroon. My study has found out that the law that regulates the functioning of the Local Governments is itself a constraint on empowerment. The utilization of the law of 1974 creating councils is a problem in Cameroon. This law was created when Cameroon operated a very tight centralized system. This period was characterised by state stronghold on all arms of government, one party politics, dictatorship and autocracy. The regulations laid down in this law depict such a system that is why councils had no autonomy, neither financial nor administrative, to engage in any activity without notification and approval from the central government. This also accounts for why there was supervision at all levels of government to ensure that the state had absolute control; from the preparation and debate of the budget to approving of a project and procuring the signature of the most immediate supervisory authority to commence a project.

The law states that a council is a decentralized political and administrative unit with legal personality and financial autonomy; yet, the budget has to go through a lot of scrutiny and then approved by the state. So, there is a lot of administrative interference. It makes no sense to vote LG representatives when in effect they are to be supervised by appointed delegates, who are more corrupt than the democratically elected administrators. All evidence points to the fact that Cameroon is still operating under a very centralized system of administration because decentralization has in effect not been accompanied by democracy and empowerment. However, one Cameroonian writes that the process of decentralization and democracy may take decades to fully implement (Tchounbia 2004).

In 1990 democracy was instituted with the introduction of multiparty politics. The democratization and decentralization processes should bring

about a completely new phase in the history of Cameroon. This phase is supposed to be accompanied by laws reflecting the new system, to meet democratic and decentralization standards, where the people are fully empowered, with less state interference because the law of 1974 is obsolete with the present circumstances. Unfortunately, this law continues to regulate the functioning of councils in Cameroon. Empowerment can only take effect when democratic values are respected – freedom of the press, free and fair elections, freedom of choice, participation, amongst others. Hence the utilization of the 1974 law of a centralized state in a decentralized democratic state presents a huge constraint to empowerment. However, it was pointed out that the law is amended and decrees passed from time to time to suit government intentions. The command-and-control measures demonstrated by Kalb (2006) to be ineffective for fostering growth has proven to be true in Buea with respect to the fact that it leaves the institutions with powers and functions that are unclear. In effect, the approach presents something completely contrary to empowerment, with ill-conceived rules and regulations that limit or impede the capacity of institutions to reach optimal expectations. It ushers to a kind of political naivety which does not necessarily apply to freedom. Therefore, while initially heralded as the magic bullet for development, most institutions fail to deliver development as promised, especially when it is infested by corruption. High quality institutions encourage trust (Kalb 2006) and make transparency the key.

The above factors illuminate the ongoing crisis in Buea that have largely contributed to Buea's socio-economic backwardness. The failure of the central government to devolve power to LG institutions and the failure to accord the local people the right to free and fair elections to choose who they desire to be their representative are accountable to the inadequacy and inefficiency in the performance of the LG. These could be considered failures of institutions to champion the course of rural development.

Implications of the Constraints on the Development of Buea

The absence of empowerment presents negative impacts on the development of Buea. When the operational and/or execution licence is given by the administration from afar (the command-and-control measure), the local people and the institutions representing them are deprived of their rights to decision making and involvement, which in turn have a negative multiplier effect on their individual lives and the municipality at large. The following are some of the consequences:

Socio-Political Exclusion

Social exclusion is a multi-dimensional, dynamic concept but it is applied here to refer to a breakdown or malfunctioning of the major societal systems that should guarantee the social integration of the individual. This includes but is not limited to the democratic and legal system which promotes civic integration. The absence of empowerment excludes the rural folk from political participation which is an exercise of their rights and freedom. Individually, the feeling of exclusion distances them from any effort towards progress in the community, and their potentials (what Sen 1999, refers to as reasoned agency) which is a contribution to the growth of the community is left unexplored, and the effect on the community is that it remains where it is, with no positive changes to eradicate poverty, fetch an income for the masses, ensure a healthy environment and attract migrants into the area who can in turn pump in money into the economy. This reduces them to unwilling actors in the political domain and this has a direct bearing on their social lives. Reducing them to second class citizens without a voice in decision making leaves them with no power to advocate for social facilities and infrastructure. This results to **poor economic performance** because the deprivation from basic social services impacts negatively on the economy of the community.

An example is the health service delivery system. A healthy population is an economically sound population because it ensures a sound work force. Citing the case of the female municipal councillor who heads the educational committee of the council, when scholarship money fails to be paid in, it impinges on the lives of those deserving pupils and students whose families cannot afford the cost of their studies. This becomes a major deficit in society as millennium goals also reflect and lay emphasis on human development to build on the capabilities of individuals in society. This poor economic performance is not only limited to human development, but covers other areas as well.

Deficiency in Infrastructure

Most of the schools in the villages in this municipality lack adequate classrooms and desks for pupils and students. The Local Government (LG) structure itself is not befitting. It is very small and tight, lacking modern devices such as computers to coordinate the system as well as store council files.

The survival of projects turns out to be shorter than the time used in their planning and establishment and albeit immense costs involved, the results are poor. This result from the fact that it is the same people that go through the same process over and over and it is the same people who have the power to decision making (that is, power revolves around the same people with the central government involved). If the state should steer clear and devolve powers to the LG to manage the affairs of its constituency and only come in at the evaluation state, the LG representatives can be judged if any deficits are realized. But unfortunately this is not the case. Sen (1999), is apt to point out that 'economic development should not only be judged in terms of growth of GNP or some other indicators of overall economic expansion, we should also look at the impact of a particular project that is put in place,

whether it is something that the people have reason to value. In the same direction, Winther (2005) indicates that a development project is not considered development per se until it is put to use by the target population. Implicitly, any project established without the consent of the people is meaningless because every project has a cultural symbol to the people and until this symbol is identified and the people cooperate it will remain a failure.

The Conclusion

The study was carried out with the following main objectives: investigating the role of the LG in socio-economic transformation particularly in rural areas in Cameroon; examination of democratic decentralization which is the force behind empowerment; and the implication of empowerment in development. The study was approached from an interdisciplinary perspective which was adopted as the best method for the study since it is a scientific method that approaches phenomena holistically. Data was fished out in two phases – primary and secondary data. Many sources of data increase the validity of results. Primary sources of data included administration of questionnaires, interviews, focus group discussions and observation. Secondary sources included books, documents, articles and vignette studies.

The results of the study revealed that the council, a decentralized unit, has achieved relatively more within the ten year period under study (1993- 2003) than during the 30 years of state-led development (1960-1990). However, assessing these achievements in relation to the population and the needs of the people, it can be concluded that the achievements and performance of the LG are inadequate and inefficient due to less autonomy and the absence of empowerment. There are other related minor factors which have contributed to the problem in Buea such as mismanagement, corruption, tribalism, and nepotism, but these are insignificant. The major problem identified from the data is persistent state grip on councils. There is decentralization in Cameroon without empowerment and this has affected development in

Buea and Cameroon in general. Some of the constraints on empowerment discussed are the utilization of a law that is supposed to be obsolete with the present system and excessive state interference, and at the

level of the council, party interests dominating common good. It is true that the LG is an arm of the government but in my opinion the government should only come to the council when the council requires help either in the form of finance or material and when the council feels a particular project is not within its competence. For example, the council would turn to the government for a permit if they have to use government property. The council may see the need to construct a befitting market for its populace in an area which is not owned by the council. It could be a government reserved area. In such a situation, the council must seek permission from the government to surrender that parcel of land and in so doing the council must submit the plan of the market and explain why they find it necessary to build that market and in that particular locality. Such are some of the instances the state should be consulted. But as long as it is within the competence of the council they should have the autonomy.

According to Nordholt (Harriss et al. 2004), the wave of decentralization that swept across many countries over the last decades meant that the maintenance of authoritarian regimes in the third world was no longer necessary, as it seemed to illustrate the failure of state led politics and projects. This is supposed to serve as a lamplight for the centre to relax its grip on regions. But, Potter (2004) purports that though the 1990s witnessed much progress towards democracy, the majority of the population of the developing world continue to live under non-elected governments. This is true in cases where elections are organised but are marred with irregularities. Democratic decentralization in

Cameroon seems more of an ideological by-product imbibed to masquerade the true picture of an authoritarian regime. It is more of a camouflage. This has resulted in particular to the lack of practical implementation of empowerment.

Though some scholars have presented with empirical evidences cases of countries that attained substantial growth in authoritarian regimes, the

literature on this only concentrates on success on economic growth but development is not only limited to economic growth. The social sector constitutes an important sector of society as the economic sector. Authoritarian regimes might have attained economic growth but not overall development if their social sectors are not developed. In some African countries purported not to have attained development in democratic regimes, some scholars have argued that it cannot be said that democracy has failed because in most countries it has never been tried (Robert and Rosberg 1985). Mawhood (1983) on his part attributes the failure of decentralization on the structure of politics. In the same line of thought, Olowu (1986) argues that the operationalization and failure of decentralization are purely conceptual, because according to him, decentralization is a convenient term that hides the true intentions of government officials. When African policy makers speak of decentralization they are actually seeking the extension of the powers and tentacles of the central government to the countryside rather than the promotion of self-governance. This is to say that African leaders are merely verbally espousing democratic ideals yet failing to implement them. This is the case of Cameroon and what is happening in Buea.

Most research focused on the comparison of authoritarian regimes and democratic regimes have come up with conclusions that the latter is the foundation for socio-economic development and vice-versa. Despite the latently promising and seemingly inclusive frameworks, LGs have failed to deliver the intended goods and services in their entirety. On the practicality of decentralization, it is widely believed to promise a range of benefits; it is suggested as a way of reducing the role and power of the state in general. Through decentralization local people can influence development policy.

In the context of Cameroon, one could say that what operates is a tight deconcentration. This is reflected in the nature in which the system operates whereby the LG is only accountable to the state and not those at the grassroots

level hence, a top-down approach. In this regard, like Ghana, Cote d'Ivoire, Kenya, Bangladesh, Mexico, Nigeria, amongst others, Cameroon is probably to be seen as an example of the failure of decentralization to meet the maximum requirements of the poor and potential to provide adequate development. (For more on failure of decentralization, see Crook and Sverrisson 2001). It fails to ensure the increased participation promised by democratic decentralization. Far from nearing its completion, democracy is still work in progress as far as Cameroon is concerned. The entire process of elections in Cameroon is seemingly a farce. Do people really have a choice? A choice where they can choose between ideologies and are not forced to opt for a corrupt regime, or where elections are not dominated by malpractices? This is very rare in Cameroon. When all political parties forget about mutual rivalries and unite to work for the betterment of Buea and Cameroon, development will attain its desired level (In the presence of empowerment and natural resources)

Democracy in Buea and in Cameroon is merely an ideological construct. The kind of political atmosphere existing in Buea is inconsistent with democratic values and development goals, and causes disunity and disintegration. This doesn't forge progress; neither does it effect social democratic change. The fundamental basis for democratic action should be communal not individualistic. The pursuit of self-interest based on conceptions of individual gain is inconsistent with democratic values and the common good (March and Olsen 1984, Spragens 1990).

Democratic transition following the second wave of political changes blowing across the continent and the rest of the developing world has not taken its toll in Cameroon. Even civic associations are viewed by the state as enemies, whereas state and civic association accord should be treated as complementary bodies and partners in the development process. Civic associations and the state should not be apart but parts of the common struggle

for the socio-economic and technological transformation of the society. This example illustrates a situation where the state only approves of establishments and public institutions where it can have a stronghold. Decentralization means empowering the LG authority, give it the power to administer in all areas be it in health centres, schools, management of roads, building of stadia, and doing a lot of infrastructure, and then the state can come and audit to ensure that there is no mismanagement, and that the LG is working to the satisfaction of the populace. Only then is it possible for the populace to have the power to send out or bring in because the LG authority will be judged within a very wide area. Placing a lot of supervision is a control mechanism and subjects the LG to a lot of dependence on the government. So, the vision of decentralization in Cameroon is very different and obscure from what the universal body politics talks about decentralization.

The economic and democratic performance in Buea is poor. There is poor state performance, that is, the transfer of authority and resources to smaller units and the common people. I therefore doubt the commitment of Cameroon to democratic standards, because corruption and mismanagement are on the increase, with Cameroon receiving the honour of dishonour of the first position as the most corrupt nation in the world according to the Transparency International Findings. Leadership and politics in developing countries especially Africa is very poor, albeit in varying degrees and that accounts for the underdeveloped status of the continent. For what I consider to be the major constraints to a democratic, decentralized system to foster the development of Buea, the following could be applied:

Revision of Council Law

There is a call to the law makers to make a revision of the 1974 law or a new law should be completely put in place to regulate the functioning of councils in Cameroon. Different systems of administration have operated in the history of Cameroon and therefore cannot operate with the same law. The law is placing a lot of control on councils which is not supposed to be the case. This cannot be attributed to ignorance, but it is a calculated strategy for the government to retain power and autonomy and this has to do with the ambiguous nature of the Cameroon constitution which gives the central government through the president unlimited powers over the state. A new law reflecting democratic and decentralization principles will devolve power to the local people and forge development. This will give the LG more autonomy to act accordingly and give the local people the right to make a choice of who to represent them, where they will have the power to cast a vote of non- confidence when the representative fails. When the LG is empowered, council funds will not have to be channelled through another institution (FEICOM). The autonomy of the LG should imply the ability to manage their resources in ways that are beneficial to the people under its jurisdiction, and then the state can come in later to evaluate their performance. But the law in place is not sufficient. Enforcement is necessary.

Enforcement of the Law

It is common practice especially in Cameroon for laws and policies to be progressive on paper. These laws need to be enforced or put into practice. To do this requires that the agencies responsible for the enforcement of laws should be strengthened and empowered to do their job effectively. Law enforcement should concentrate on some indicators of good governance. One such indicator could be transparency.

Transparency

Transparency should be the key at both local and national levels. Transparency should also be encouraged both in giving accounts of actions to those represented and in elections. There should be transparency in the electoral system, so as to regain the confidence of the population. When elections are free and fair, the people take responsibility for their choice of representative. This increases their level of participation and commitment which depicts a true politically decentralized system. There is therefore the need to create more open political environments in which citizens can actively participate in the democratic process. In other words, there is need for the advancement of democratic values, practices and institutions. Good governance is not only limited to transparency, it requires continuity.

Continuity

It has been found in my study that there is no institutional continuity. The council fails to operate as an institution, but as an individual or party entity. This means that people follow party lines, instead of a continuous process, where one regime continues from where the other stops. The abandonment of projects initiated and started by a previous regime is a waste of resources. It would be better to concentrate on one project at a time and see that it is effectively executed so that attention can be focused on another. These representatives come and go but the council stays. What is important is the achievements of the council, not of an individual. Belonging to opposing political parties is not a reason good enough to constitute a crisis in development efforts. Development should be a joint action, reflecting the well-being of the local people.

Above all, councils should operate independent treasuries as long as these funds are raised by councils. It is inappropriate for councils to raise funds and these funds are managed by the state. Moreover, when councils run

short of funds to execute projects, the government should give subventions to councils from government coffers to ensure that development is attained at the grassroots. Long term projects should also be encouraged instead of short term projects that need to be repeated after a short period. Other suggestions as to what can be done to improve on the lives of the people of Buea in the presence of empowerment include:

Diversification of the Economy

Buea is an area that is blessed with natural resources that can permit it to diversify its economy. For example, Buea has the potential to attract Cameroonians and foreigners alike. Every place in the world has its unique advantages. For the mere fact that Buea is not an industrial area and may not be that for a long time, it should take advantage of its natural endowments and forge the progress of the area. Buea is blessed with a wonderful climate in relation to the rest of the country and has wonderful opportunities for a diversified economy. If these opportunities are exploited it would pull a lot of people who would be ready to come and spend money. This would in turn create employment opportunities for the local people and hence make Buea a better place. Hence, other livelihood strategies should be exploited such as tourism.

Involvement of the Civil Society and other development agents

The information collected from the field reveals that the council is 'state run' and is not responding favourably to the needs of the rural people. Since the council seems to be acting as an armchair of the central government, the non public sector within the municipality should take it as a task to develop Buea either in collaboration with the council (as a partner) or independently (in case the council refuses to cooperate). This means that the task of developing Buea should not also be solely that of the council. The civil society (groups of

people who associate voluntarily to advance common interests e.g. NGOs) should mobilize the population for different productive activities, source funding for development projects, provide employment, carry out social projects, serve as agents of civic education by increasing the public's understanding of issues at stake, manage projects for the council as joint venture or on lease, and above all, promote the culture of the people in the municipality. Non- public actors can help build the capacity of councils and facilitate access to development by funding development needs, and they can empower the community. If this is done, Buea will in no time become a place worth its status.

In all, few studies have concentrated or embarked on whether power has been devolved in Cameroon with the implementation of political decentralization. Public institutions such as Local Governments are persistently failing to touch adequately on grassroots needs; yet, other explanations have often dominated the debate. The results of this study are therefore generalizable to other areas in Cameroon and this study should serve as a prelude or a call for in-depth case studies on this issue. Among other elements or factors pointed out to constitute the challenges and deficiencies in the operationalization of the LG in Buea, the most crucial are at the level of the central government. This requires that future research should concentrate on this area. These include the laws of the country which perpetuates excessive state grip on institutions and corrupt government officials. These should serve as a fundamental point of departure for future researchers.

Although some authoritarian regimes have recorded remarkable successes in development, and though empowerment might not necessarily be a guarantee to development, I concede that it is very necessary especially if implemented in its fullness and with all intent. I hope this study provides a useful guide and stimulus for further research into the topic.

www.ingramcontent.com/pod-product-compliance
Lightning Source LLC
Chambersburg PA
CBHW031106080526
44587CB00011B/853